I0079726

The Least of These

*The Role of Good Deeds
In a Jesus-Shaped Spirituality*

By R. Maurice Smith

RISING RIVER MEDIA

© **Copyright 2011, 2014. Rising River Media.**
All rights reserved.

2014 Revised Edition

Written permission must be secured from the publisher to use or reproduce any part of this work in any form except where quotations are accompanied by a full and accurate recitation of the work's full title, the publisher, and the publisher's address. Additional copies of this publication are available from the address given below:

Published by Rising River Media, P. O. Box 9133, Spokane, Washington 99209

www.risingrivermedia.org

Cover Art, *"My Brother's Keeper"*
Original Watercolor by Laurie Goldstein-Warren
Used under license.
© Copyright Laurie Goldstein-Warren. All rights Reserved.
http://www.warrenwatercolors.com/

Unless otherwise noted, all Scripture quotations are from The Holy Bible, English Standard Version (ESV), Copyright 2001 by Crossway Bibles, a publishing ministry of Good News Publishers. Used by permission. All rights reserved.

ISBN 13   978-0-9960096-4-5

Other Titles Available From Rising River Media

And They Dreamt Of A Kingdom
Biblical Reflections On Discipleship And The Kingdom Of God - Volume 1

All Dogs Go To Heaven, Don't They?
Biblical Reflections On Christian Universalism and Ultimate Reconciliation

Preparing For The Coming Spiritual Outpouring
Reflections On The Coming Move of God's Spirit

River Houses Rising
The Rise of Safe Houses Of Hope And Prayer

Safe Houses of Hope And Prayer
Your Practical Guide To Organic Church In Your House

The Inextinguishable Blaze
God's Call To Holiness, Repentance, Intimacy and Spiritual Awakening

When Jesus Visits His Church
A Study Of The Seven Churches of Asia (Revelation Chapters 2-3)

You Wanna Do What In Your House?!
Straight Answers To Your Most Frequently Asked Questions About House Church

All titles are available on our website at *www.risingrivermedia.org* from Amazon.com!

Table of Contents

To our dear friends,

Art and Linda Fried

without whose support and encouragements
over the years, our ministry among "the least of these"
would not have been possible. Thank you.

Author's Preface
To The Revised Edition

I had just returned from attending my daughter's graduation from Princeton Theological Seminary in New Jersey. My older brother and I had gone to the Raleigh Durham Airport to rent a car for the remainder of my 10-day stay with family in North Carolina. As the woman behind the rental car counter tapped away on her computer to complete our paperwork my brother commented to her concerning my work among the poor in Spokane. At that point, a strange thing happened. The lovely lady behind the counter began to weep. It seems that she had come out of an abusive marriage. In the process she and her son had been homeless and forced to live in her car for a while. Now, she was back on her feet and had been asking God if He had anything for her to do among people who were struggling. I had recently completed the original edition of this book and gave her a complimentary copy. The next day I received an e-mail from her through our website. Here's what she wrote:

"I cannot tell you how deeply our conversation at the ***** Car Rental counter touched me today. I went to my car at lunch, began reading your book and wept. I wept and could not understand why until it hit me. Relief. Hearing the plans you and your brother have for the homeless here in Wake county felt like someone had finally heard what my heart has been screaming for so long. It was honestly overwhelming.

"As a child of missionaries, I have lived among the poorest of the poor in countries over seas. As an adult I have come to realize that we need not go abroad to find those in similar

The Least Of These

circumstances. Those who are the invisible nation within a nation. Those for whom my heart breaks. A broken heart is not enough, the question has been what exactly can I do? I can feed one, maybe two when I can. Find suppliers who will provide free medication for this person or that one. It just hasn't seemed like enough. There is so much more to be done. I have been praying for guidance, for some way to make a difference. I'm ashamed to say I had all but given up...and then two brothers walk in to a car rental agency....sounds like a joke doesn't it? God knows what He is doing.

"Thank you for your kind words today. For your book, for giving voice and action to the deepest pull of my heart. Thank you for not only seeing the "invisible" but loving them. I am honored to have met you and now I feel that I have the confirmation I need that the call I have heard for years is not my own voice. I may be broken and wounded, but I am willing to answer that call. Thank you again. S*****"

Christian philosopher and apologist Ravi Zacharias has posed the question of our day, namely, how do we effectively reach out with the love of God to a generation of people who *"listen with their eyes and think with their feelings"*? I believe that a significant part of the answer to that question is: *"through our good deeds."* The goal of this book is to help you understand the Scriptural importance of good deeds in the life of the believer and to encourage you, like the woman at the car rental agency, to answer that call.

Maurice Smith
October, 2014

Introduction

Her name was Margie. My wife and I were on a writing sabbatical, staying with friends in Maui, when I ran into Margie at the local McDonalds on South Kihei Road (across from Long's Drug Store). I had gone there for my morning caffè latte, to mooch their free Wi-Fi and to work on some writing. As I waited for my order I saw Margie standing close by to one side, counting her change. Having worked with homeless and disadvantaged people for several years, I quickly surmised Margie's situation and understood that she was trying to see if she had enough change to order something.

"How much is it for a cup of coffee?" she asked no one in particular. Taking that as my cue, I responded.

"What would you like?" I asked as I stepped closer to her.

"Well, I wanted to get something to eat . . ." she said, her words trailing off in an unfinished sentence toward an unspoken conclusion.

"Would you mind if I bought you breakfast?" I asked. And without pausing to explore the surprise on her face, I continued. *"Come on,"* I said, gently leading her to an available cashier. *"My friend would like a big breakfast and something to drink,"* I told the cashier. A knowing look and a smile from the cashier told me she, too, understood what was happening. It's the "ripple effect" of a good deed in a public

The Least Of These

setting.

Margie and I got her order and headed toward the seating area. A flurry of taunts and cat-calls from three scruffy men at a close-by table told me that Margie was not alone.

"What ya doin', Margie? Did you tell 'im you're HIV positive, Margie?" I had already surmise all of that.

"What difference does that make?" I snapped back. *"She's hungry!"* Patience with a senseless lack of kindness is not one of my gifts.

I got Margie settled at a table where she could enjoy breakfast in peace and assured her that God loved her. And as I walked away reflecting on what had just unfolded I was reminded that sometimes the Kingdom of God and the love of the King look like a kind stranger and taste like a hot breakfast.

". . . to the extent that you did it to one of these brothers of Mine, even the least of them, you did it to Me."

Welcome to good deeds and their role in a Jesus-shaped spirituality, a spirituality which looks like Jesus and sounds like the Kingdom of God. And one of the unmistakable characteristics of such a Jesus-shaped spirituality is its commitment to good deeds, especially toward those whom Jesus referred to as *"the least of these."*

The focus of this book is on one specific characteristic of a Jesus-shaped spirituality, namely, the role of what Scripture refers to as good deeds. But in order to put things into some

Introduction

contemporary perspective I will begin our journey together by challenging what I refer to as the religion-shaped spirituality of the contemporary Evangelical church. It is a spirituality that is first and foremost *"attractional"* rather than *"incarnational,"* terms we will examine more closely in Chapters 1 and 2. The motto of this religion-shaped spirituality is, *"If you build it and offer enough attractive programs, they will come."* In its place I want to examine the idea of a Jesus-shaped spirituality by looking at the spirituality of Jesus Himself and its relationship to good deeds. We will do this in Chapter 3. Next, I will take us on extended journey through the New Testament in order to see what it has to say about the importance of good deeds in the life of the believer (Chapter 4). This will be followed by an examination of two additional and important passages of Scripture which impact our understanding of God's call upon each of us to minister to *"the least of these"* (Chapters 5 and 6). In Chapter 7 we will respond to a couple of frequently asked questions concerning good deeds, namely, who should be the object of our good deeds (believers or unbelievers), and are good deeds optional for the believer. The next two Chapters (8 and 9) will contain several stories of good deeds that I have either been personally involved with, or which have come to me from people I am in personal contact with. Finally, we will conclude our journey together with a challenge for all of us to "become legendary" in our pursuit of good deeds and a Jesus-shaped spirituality.

How We Understand Scripture

As evangelical Christians, our understanding of life and godliness is shaped by our understanding of Scripture. Indeed, we can say that our faith rests upon three things: the

The Least Of These

nature of God, the person and work of Christ and the inspired teaching of Scripture.

But what we glean from a text of Scripture - and what we apply in our lives - often depends upon something as mundane as which translation we use. It's one of the drawbacks of having a sacred text which was originally written in a language (1st Century Greek) other than our native tongue. We must rely upon the translations of others which often vary. Consider the four translations of Revelation 22:12 given below. The first one is my original translation of the Greek text, while the other three are contemporary versions of the same passage.

"Behold, I am coming quickly, and My wage is with Me to give to each according to his deeds." (Revelation 22:12, author's translation)

"Yes, I'm on my way! I'll be there soon! I'm bringing my payroll with me. I'll pay all people in full for their life's work." (Revelation 22:12 from The Message).

"Behold, I am coming quickly, and My reward is with Me, to render to every man according to what he has done." (Revelation 22:12 New American Standard Bible, 1977)

"Behold, I am coming soon, bringing my recompense with me, to repay everyone for what he has done." (Revelation 22:12 English Standard Version)

Do you see any differences? And could those differences change the way you understand the passage and your

Introduction

application of its teaching in your own life? Let me suggest a couple of differences I noticed. **First,** let's look at the Greek word *misthos*. In the 1st Century Greek of the New Testament this was the common

> *". . . Jesus will one day return to His vineyard and 'pay a wage' to each individual laborer."*

word for a day's wage earned by a common laborer. But these four translations use four different words: "wage" (Author's); "reward" (NASB); "payroll" (Message); "recompense" (ESV). While all are acceptable translations, "wage" is a more precise description. **Second,** the phrase translated *"what he has done"* literally reads *"as his deed is."* That's good Greek, but it's poor English, so we smooth it out to read *"according to his deeds."* The word "deed" is the common word used throughout the New Testament for all "deeds," whether good or evil.[1]

O.K., there really is a point to all of this linguistic wrangling. I would dare say that most contemporary professing Christians have no real clue that, in some real sense we don't fully grasp, Jesus sees us as day laborers in His vineyard. According to this passage, and many others we will examine in the course of this book, Jesus will one day return to His vineyard and *"pay a wage"* to each of us, based on the work ("deeds") each of us performed while in His employ. Or to be a bit more specific, how you and I treated the "Margies" of this world. So, what kind of employee have you been, and

---

[1]The Greek word *ergon* can also be translated "work," but in the interest of consistency and avoiding confusion we are rendering it consistently as "deed."

The Least Of These

what "wage" have you earned?

Snoopy's Two Simple Goals

In the early 1960s a fellow by the name of Robert Short was a struggling Seminary student at the University of Chicago Divinity School. Looking for a way to support himself and pay his school bills, he hit on the idea of taking one of the most popular comic strips of the day and writing about the theological lessons it contained. In 1965 his book, **The Gospel According To Peanuts**, appeared in bookstores, and Robert Short was able to pay his school bills (now having sold over 15 million copies). Among his many observations, Short suggested that the character of *Snoopy* in the beloved comic strip *"Peanuts"* represented the Christ character, whose role was to comfort the afflicted, and to afflict the comfortable.

My two goals for this book resemble Short's understanding of Snoopy. My first goal is to comfort and encourage those of you who have already embraced the truth of Scripture concerning the role of good deeds in a Jesus-shaped spirituality. You are the "shining lights" of the Church and the Kingdom of God. It is because of you that men *"glorify your Father who is in heaven."* This book is my encouragement to you to keep up the "good works."

My second goal is equally simple. I want to afflict the rest of you. Sorry, it's a gift and I can't seem to help myself. My goal is to prick your conscience, to challenge your comfort and to

Introduction

"incite" [2] you to *"greater love and good deeds"* (Hebrews 10: 23-25). This is your call, the call of the organic house church movement and the call of professing Christians everywhere to walk in a Jesus-shaped spirituality and to become "legendary" for our good deeds.

What happens next is up to you.

---

[2]The Greek word *paroxusmos* communicates the idea of provoking or irritating someone to the point of "inciting" them to action.

The Least Of These

"Do all the good you can, by all the means you can, in all the ways you can, in all the places you can, at all the times you can, to all the people you can, as long as you can."

- John Wesley, Founder of The Methodist Church

"Our Postmodern culture has concluded that it can manifest 'good deeds' without Jesus. The Church has concluded that it can manifest Jesus without 'good deeds.' Our Postmodern culture's plan appears to be working. The Church's plan is a disaster."

- Author

The Least Of These

Chapter 1

Jesus and Hula Hoops

Americans are a fad-driven people. Whether it's hula hoops, silly putty, pet rocks or cabbage patch babies, we are incorrigible fad-followers with short attention spans. Unfortunately, the same is often true of the Evangelical Church in America. We don't call our activities "fads." We refer to them as "programs," and in my 40-plus years in the Church I have been through countless local programs and several national ones: Here's Life, Atlanta!, Here's Life, America! Here's Life, World!, Key '73, Evangelism Explosion, Operation World, Basic Youth Conflicts, Shepherding, The Purpose Driven Life, The Purpose Driven Church, 40 Days of Purpose, megachurch mania, seeker sensitive services, and more that I could list but won't. Hopefully, we get the point.

The Church in America is nearly as fad driven as our culture. We seem incapable of doing anything without a program. Think of it as a religious fad. We like to ask, *"What would Jesus do?"* But our answer is almost always that He would create a new program for 40 days of something-or-the-other complete with a book, CD/DVD, study guide and matching bracelet. As I mentioned in the *Introduction*, my wife and I recently took a personal writing sabbatical to Maui, Hawaii as the guests of Christian friends. In a Christian book store there I discovered a display offering "faith rocks." I quipped to my wife that apparently someone with a warehouse full of "pet rocks" had finally figured out how to get rid of them! And

The Least Of These

my mind immediately turned again to hula hoops. *"Jesus Hoops,"* I mused. *"There's got to be a market out there for 'Jesus Hoops.'"*

"It was never the heart of God or the mission of Jesus to raise up a religious people."

The Church in America is driven by many things. But at the end of the day, as the sun sets on another day of ceaseless activity, the question we really need to ask - but seldom do - is this: *"Are we Jesus-driven?"* The long-term result of our religious fads and programs is that we have created a personal spirituality that is shaped by many other things, including religion and church, rather than being shaped by Jesus. Indeed, a Jesus-shaped spirituality is becoming increasingly rare.

The Mission of Jesus

"As He hung on the cross Jesus probably never thought the impact of his sacrifice would be reduced to an invitation for people to join and to support an institution." [3]

It was never the heart of God or the mission of Jesus to raise up a religious people. Camp on that thought for just a moment and let it sink in. When Jesus came to earth during the reign of Augustus Caesar, the land of Palestine was already filled with religious people. They worshiped daily in the Temple in Jerusalem and on every Sabbath in hundreds

---

[3]Reggie McNeal, **The Present Future: Six Tough Questions for the Church** (San Francisco: John Wiley & Sons, 2003), Page1.

Jesus And Hula Hoops

of synagogues scattered throughout the land of Israel. Their leaders debated theology, divided themselves into competing sects, studied the sacred Scriptures, argued politics, and made public displays of their personal piety. I don't know if they sponsored any "programs."

No. God neither needed nor wanted more religious people. He had plenty of those to spare. The landscape of Palestine was littered with them. The Judaism of Jesus' day had degenerated from a Jehovah-shaped spirituality

"Jesus never once challenged any of His would-be disciples to be religious, to join a synagogue or even to start a church."

to a religion-shaped spirituality which had turned the 612 requirements of the Old Testament Law into over 5,000 religious rules and expectations (known as the *"traditions of the elders"*) which governed the religious life of Ancient Israel and held the people of God in religious bondage. It was the mission of Jesus to change that.

As He undertook His all-too-brief three year ministry and called His disciples to Himself, Jesus never once challenged any of His would-be disciples to be religious, to join a synagogue or even to start a church. He simply challenged them to follow him . . . and to learn. When the disciples of John the Baptist asked Jesus, *"Where are you staying?,"* He didn't give them a set of directions. He simply challenged them to *"Come and see"* (John 1:38-39). They would come. They would see. And they would be forever changed by what

23

The Least Of These

they saw.[4] Up to this point in their lives they had seen the religion-shaped spirituality of the rabbis and scribes, the Pharisees and Sadducees. But they now saw something very different. They saw the Jehovah-shaped spirituality of a carpenter from Nazareth Who chose not to associate with religious leaders or the rich and powerful, but with the spiritually poor, the dispossessed and the marginalized; one who could heal lepers with a touch and still a raging storm with a word. And life for those twelve men would never be the same.

For His part, Jesus' desire was to establish a spiritual Kingdom, populated with disciples whose distinguishing characteristic would be a spirituality formed and

> "A Jesus-shaped spirituality stands out, like a spiritual round peg in a world dominated by religious square ones."

shaped around Himself. For three-and-a-half years He model it for them to imitate, and later to duplicate. By the time He returned to His Father, Jesus left a handful of men who manifested a Jesus-shaped spirituality. And disciples with a Jesus-shaped spirituality stand out. So much so that when the Jewish religious authorities later examined the disciples in Acts 4 they were stumped to explain their uniqueness until they realized that these were men who had been with Jesus. *"Now when they saw the boldness of Peter and John, and perceived that they were uneducated, common men, they*

---

[4]We examine Jesus' call of His disciples in greater detail in our book *And They Dreamt Of A Kingdom: Biblical Reflections On Discipleship And The Kingdom of God - Volume 1*, available on our website from Amazon.com. See particularly *"Chapter 9 - Beginnings."*

Jesus And Hula Hoops

were astonished. And they recognized that they had been with Jesus" (Acts 4:13). A Jesus-shaped spirituality stands out, like a spiritual round peg in a world dominated by religious square ones.[5]

The same was true when the early Church took root in Antioch, *."* . . . .*and the disciples were first called Christians in Antioch"* (Acts 11:26). We don't know who first referred to the disciples in Antioch as "Christians" in

> *"They accused them of looking like Jesus. They accused them of manifesting a Jesus-shaped spirituality."*

Acts 11. I suspect it was people outside the Church who intended the label as something approaching a slur. The Greek phrase is a diminutive meaning "little-Christ-ones." If so, they unwittingly paid those early disciples the highest possible compliment. They accused them of looking like Jesus. They accused them of manifesting a Jesus-shaped spirituality.

From Purpose Driven To Jesus Driven

Please don't get me wrong. I really don't care what you think about hula hoops, pet rocks, faith rocks, purpose driven churches or any other fads or church programs. But more importantly, I don't think our Postmodern culture cares either. Hula hoops appear to be out of favor (again), and so do

---

[5]For a more extensive development of a Jesus-Shaped Spirituality, see Chapter 8 of our book, *River Houses Rising: The Rise of Safe Houses of Hope And Prayer*, available on our website from Amazon.com.

The Least Of These

purpose driven, seeker friendly churches. For the most part, unbelievers have come to our mega-services, sipped our lattes, watched our multi-media productions and have left unimpressed and asking, *"Is that all you've got?"* They came looking for a Jesus-shaped spirituality among a community of professing believers, and what they found was another religious program on steroids . . . and mediocre coffee.[6]

The evangelical church in America and the West is in serious need of a wake-up call that will shake us out of our religious boxes and challenge both our religion-shaped spirituality and our

> *"We have become complacent in the midst of an on-going catastrophe."*

Laodicean lethargy. We have become complacent in the midst of an on-going catastrophe. Our "attractional" model of Church simply isn't working to any noticeable degree. Despite all of our seeker-friendly church growth efforts over the past generation, church attendance in America has fallen dramatically, from 42% of adults in 1965 to as low as 20% today. The *"Ship of Church"* is listing badly, but few seem willing to acknowledge the problem, much less address it. As Michael Spencer adroitly observed, Evangelical Christians seem to believe - indeed, they insist - that *"their ship is listing to one side because it gives them a more interesting look at*

---

[6]While this might seem harsh, the reality of this has been documented by such books as Jim Henderson and Matt Casper, *Jim and Casper Go to Church: Frank Conversation about Faith, Churches, and Well-Meaning Christians* (Ventura, CA: Barna Books, 2007).

the iceberg."[7]

A Manifesto, Of Sorts

This book is a manifesto of sorts - an integral part of a larger apologetic for a new spiritual paradigm which involves five basic commitments: [8]

A Commitment to Revival and Spiritual Awakening. Throughout church history, when the *"Ship of Church"* has found itself listing badly, God has heard the desperate cries of His people and has and responded with seasons of profound spiritual renewal and revival. That's where we find ourselves today - listing badly and in need of divine intervention. And it is for this reason that we are committed to the vision of a coming spiritual awakening, an end-time harvest of historic proportions, which will sweep millions of people into the Kingdom of God.

A Commitment to Spirit Led Organic House Churches. We are committed to a vision of organic house churches as the new channel or vessel through which that spiritual awakening will flow. God is raising up a new wineskin for the new wine of this coming harvest, a wineskin consisting of tens of thousands of organic house churches where the focus is

---

[7]Michael Spencer, *Mere Churchianity: Finding Your Way Back To Jesus-Shaped Spirituality* (Waterbrook Multnomah: New York, 2010), page 23.

[8]We explore this new paradigm in much greater detail in two of our books, *River Houses Rising* and *Safe Houses of Hope And Prayer*. Both are available on our website from Amazon.com.

The Least Of These

upon holiness and the fear of God, personal repentance, genuine worship, personal discipleship, biblical community and local outreach.

A Commitment to Fasting And Prayer. It is impossible to separate personal discipleship, biblical spirituality or even Church from the biblical disciplines of fasting and prayer. Jesus never said *"if you pray"* or *"if you fast."* It was never about "if." It was always about "when" (See Matthew 6:1-18). The practical reality of this spiritual truth is that every historic spiritual revival in the Church for the past 300 years has been preceded by periods of prolonged personal and corporate prayer and fasting. For this reason we have a strong commitment to personal and corporate fasting and prayer.

A Commitment to Discipleship as the Life-long Pursuit of a Jesus-shaped Spirituality. We are committed to organic house church as the regular gathering of believers in the common pursuit of a Jesus-shaped spirituality; a spirituality that looks like Jesus and sounds like the Kingdom of God. New Testament spirituality has never been about where

> *"Biblical faith, from Jesus' day until our day, has always been about what it means to be 'a disciple of the Kingdom'."*

people meet (i.e., in "sacred buildings") or when people meet (i.e., on a "sacred day") or even what they "do" when they meet (i.e., engage in "religious activity"). Biblical faith, from Jesus' day until our day, has always been about what it means to be *"a disciple of the Kingdom"* (Matthew 13:52). We believe that to be a *"disciple of the Kingdom"* means to make it our life's goal to actively pursue the Kingdom of God

Jesus And Hula Hoops

through the development of a Jesus-shaped spirituality within a community of like-minded believers who gather for the purpose of equipping, building and encouraging one another in their common pursuit of Christ-likeness.[9]

A Commitment to Good Deeds and Serving "The Least of These." We are committed to a spiritual paradigm characterized by incarnational ministry and good deeds, particularly toward *"the least of these."* When was the last time you personally fed the hungry, clothed the naked, befriended the stranger, visited the prisoner or engaged in any of the good deeds described in Matthew 25: 35-36 as a personal expression of your faith and your commitment to the Kingdom of God? We are committed to a spiritual paradigm which takes seriously the New Testament teaching on the importance of good deeds in the life of the believer.

And that is the topic of the remainder of this book.

---

[9]Again, we explore what it means to be a "disciple of the Kingdom" in much greater detail in our book *And They Dreamt Of A Kingdom*, available on our website from Amazon.com.

The Least Of These

Chapter 2

Whatever Happened To Incarnational Truth?

"Most of us have a spirituality which has been formed by the lukewarm church of Laodicea, rather than the bold counter-cultural church of Smyrna." - Michael Spencer

A Personal Journal
Into A Jesus-Shaped Spirituality

My own pursuit of a Jesus-shaped spirituality has led me into many places I never intended to go. To begin with it led me out of the institutional church I had known all of my life and into the organic house church movement. It also led me into desperate drug infested neighborhoods in our city to share the love of Christ and to work with the very people whom I believe Jesus referred to as *"the least of these."* My pursuit of a Jesus-shaped spirituality led me to organize a food rescue agency and to serve as its Executive Director for five years, in order to find and provide the food necessary to feed the hungry of our community (more about that in Chapter 9). And my pursuit of a Jesus-shaped spirituality led me to volunteer at a local men's homeless shelter, where my wife and I now serve on the Board of Directors. In the process, God taught me to work with a wide variety of people I had never considered or met before, because the purveyors of my religion-shaped spirituality had told me to avoid them. Jesus told me to love them, and to model His love to them.

Finally, my pursuit of a Jesus-shaped spirituality forced me

The Least Of These

to ask and to answer questions I had never asked before. One of those questions, which became the theme of this book, had to do with the role of what Scripture refers to as good deeds in any Jesus-shaped spirituality. I was aghast to realize that in all

> *"Jesus, the non-created second person of the triune God-head, took on a human body and nature and walked the earth as both fully man and fully God."*

of my years of seminary, bible study and teaching, I had never examined what the Bible has to say about good deeds or what my responsibility might be as a follower of Jesus to practice good deeds. This book represents my personal wrestling with that question. My goal is to force you to wrestle with it, too. What answers you arrive at will be up to you.

From Attractional To Incarnational

"And the Word became flesh, and dwelt among us, and we beheld His glory, glory as of the only begotten from the Father, full of grace and truth." John 1:14

I suppose that in order for this chapter to make sense, a quick definition is in order. The word "Incarnation" or "Incarnate" derives from two Latin phrases (*in* = in or into, *caro*, *carnis* = flesh) meaning *"to make into flesh"* or *"to become flesh."* As a doctrine, the Incarnation is a fundamental theological teaching of orthodox (Nicene) Christianity, namely, that Jesus, the non-created second person of the triune God-head, took on a human body and nature and walked the earth as both fully man and fully God.

Whatever Happened To Incarnational Truth?

He became "incarnate" and undertook an existence and a ministry which was "incarnational." Or as the writer John, who walked with Jesus, describes it (in Maurice's paraphrase of the Greek text), *"the divine Word clothed himself in human flesh and temporarily pitched His tent among us, and we saw it."*

"Incarnational Christianity leaves its comfortable and elaborate boxes and seeks to "pitch its tent" among those who most need to hear the good news of the Kingdom of God."

In their excellent book, **The Shaping of Things To Come: Innovation and Mission for the 21st Century Church**, authors Frost and Hirsh discuss the difference between what they call "Attractional Christianity," and "Incarnational Christianity." On the one hand, Attractional Christianity builds elaborate boxes and sponsors elaborate programs in the hope of attracting curious unbelievers. Attractional Christianity is purpose-driven, seeker-friendly and invitational (*"We want to invite you to come see our amazing drama presentation and hear our amazing worship band, etc., etc."*). On the other hand, Incarnational Christianity leaves its comfortable and elaborate boxes and seeks to "pitch its tent" among those who most need to hear the good news of the Kingdom of God. Frost and Hirsh stress the need for the Church to move from being attractional (attracting people to come to our outstanding programs) to being "incarnational," taking the Kingdom of God out to where people are, and on terms which they understand.

The Least Of These

In an earlier ground breaking book author Leonard Sweet declared that the organized Church needed to become "EPIC."[10] He argued that in our Postmodern culture the organized Church needed to adopt four primary characteristics. In order to be more attractional the Church needed to become experiential, participatory, image-driven and community-building. The ink was scarcely dry on the printed page before this had been interpreted to mean that churches needed state of the art sound and video systems, stages for plays rather than pulpits, snappy PowerPoint visuals, contemporary music and a bistro.

But when all was said and done, EPIC church had become little more than traditional attractional church on steroids. . . plus a bistro. While none of these things are bad or wrong (please read that statement AGAIN!) they miss the point. The point and the problem was that even EPIC churches were (and are) still based upon an attractional model of Christianity rather than an incarnational one. But worse, it continued the pattern of teaching and modeling an institution-based, religion-shaped spirituality in an age when an increasing number of people, both inside and outside the Church, are looking for something more: The personal incarnation of a Jesus-shaped spirituality.[11]

---

[10]Leonard Sweet, *Post Modern Pilgrims: First Century Passion for the 21st Century Church* (Nashville: Broadman & Holman, 2000).

[11]My thinking on this issue has been deeply affected by the writings of Michael Spencer in his one and only book, *Mere Churchianity: Finding Your Way Back To Jesus-Shaped Spirituality* (Waterbrook Multnomah: New York, 2010). Michael passed away in April of 2010. I hope he discovered this book to be a crown.

Whatever Happened To Incarnational Truth?

"Soup, Soap & Salvation"

Incarnational ministry is not new. John Wesley was forced to adopt an incarnational ministry in England of the 1750s. When churches throughout London and elsewhere closed their doors to Wesley and his evangelical message, he took his message to the mines, fields and streets of England where the people were, irrespective of parish boundaries, a radical notion in his day, leading to Wesley's motto that *"The world is my parish."* Under Wesley's direction and tutelage the early Methodists became legendary for their incarnational work among the poor and destitute of London. When it came to good deeds and incarnational ministry, Wesley's philosophy was simple:

"Do all the good you can, by all the means you can, in all the ways you can, in all the places you can, at all the times you can, to all the people you can, as long as you can."

Later, in the mid-1800s, when William and Catherine Booth found it nearly impossible to reach the mass of slum dwellers in London from within traditional mainstream Methodism (which since Wesley's day had become

> *"Incarnational ministry is not new in the history of the Church. We simply tend to forget how to do it, or why it is so important."*

increasingly "attractional") they left and founded the Salvation Army. Through their "incarnational" ministry on the streets of London and throughout England they became known for their social work and for their street motto: *"Soup, Soap and*

The Least Of These

Salvation." Incarnational ministry is not new in the history of the Church. We simply tend to forget how to do it, or why it is so important.

What Would Jesus Do?

As we observed earlier, while the EPIC model of Church has been widely adopted by many contemporary Churches, it continues to rely upon an attractional model of Christianity, as opposed to an incarnational one. It still promotes a religion-shaped spirituality rather than a Jesus-shaped spirituality. As a result, to suggest that Christians and Churches today STILL need to move from an attractional model of ministry to an incarnational model of ministry remains a revolutionary notion. Why? Because it is a declaration that even our EPIC model of attractional Christianity isn't working despite the vast resources Churches have invested. It is a declaration that our church-based, religion-shaped spirituality has failed and it is time to change. It is time to pursue a new form of Church and a Jesus-shaped spirituality that is rarely seen or practiced today.

". . . it is a declaration that even our EPIC model of attractional Christianity isn't working despite the vast resources Churches have invested."

To actively pursue a Jesus-shaped spirituality as opposed to a religion-shaped spirituality is a radical concept for most contemporary religion-bound Christians. It challenges all of our religious comfort zones and forces us to ask ourselves,

Whatever Happened To Incarnational Truth?

"What would Jesus do in this situation?" rather than *"What has my church or denomination or seminary taught me to do in this situation?"* As revolutionary as this thought might be, ours is not the first generation of believers to wrestle with the question of *"What would Jesus do?"* And that's a story we need to tell.

In His Steps

In the 1890s Charles Sheldon was a Congregational pastor in Topeka, Kansas. He delivered a series of sermons to his congregation which later appeared in print as a serial in the *Chicago Advance*, a religious weekly publication. As a result, the book, ***In His Steps: What Would Jesus Do?,*** was not only born, but was thrown into the "public domain" because the publisher didn't understand copyright law. In simple terms, no one had legal rights to the story, so publishers all over the world released the book. By 1935 the book had been translated into 21 languages and was a recognized best seller. Today it is regarded as a Christian Classic.

In the novel, the lead character, Reverend Henry Maxwell, encounters a homeless man who has difficulty understanding why, in his view, so many Christians ignore the poor:

"I heard some people singing at a church prayer meeting the other night,
'All for Jesus, all for Jesus,
All my being's ransomed powers,
All my thoughts, and all my doings,
All my days, and all my hours.'
"and I kept wondering as I sat on the steps outside just what

The Least Of These

they meant by it. It seems to me there's an awful lot of trouble in the world that somehow wouldn't exist if all the people who sing such songs went and lived them out. I suppose I don't understand. But what would Jesus do? Is that what you mean by following His steps? It seems to me sometimes as if the people in the big churches had good clothes and nice houses to live in, and money to spend for luxuries, and could go away on summer vacations and all that, while the people outside the churches, thousands of them, I mean, die in tenements, and walk the streets for jobs, and never have a piano or a picture in the house, and grow up in misery and drunkenness and sin."

Reverend Maxwell is deeply moved by this encounter and is challenged to take his Christianity more seriously by imitating Jesus. He goes on to challenge the members of his congregation to face every situation in their lives by asking themselves *"What would Jesus do?"* (O.K., if you want to know how it all turns out, you'll need to read the book. It is a classic, and a worthwhile read!).

Now, fast forward to 1989. Janie Tinklenberg was serving as youth leader at Calvary Reformed Church in Holland, Michigan when she decided to re-read Sheldon's **In His Steps**. She began to discuss the idea of *"What would Jesus do?"* with her youth group. *"I prodded them to consider this question, 'How do we make ethical and moral judgments about who we are as a people of faith?' I wanted the young people to understand that we have a standard - Jesus."* [12]

---

[12]Sandy Sheppard, *"What Would Jesus Do?"* © Christianity Today International, posted online at www.christianity.com/Christian%20Living/Features/11622298/.

Whatever Happened To Incarnational Truth?

Reflecting on the popularity of "friendship bracelets" and "wait-until-marriage" rings, Tinklenberg had an idea. She contacted Mike Freestone of Lesco Corporation in Holland, Michigan and asked about producing bracelets with the letters WWJD (an acronym for "What Would Jesus Do?"). *"The bracelets had a two-fold purpose,"* she said. *"First, I wanted the young people to be reminded, every time they looked at the bracelet, of the commitment [to Christ] they made. Second, the bracelet could be a tool for witnessing to friends."*

The popularity of the bracelets slowly grew as more and more youth gave the bracelets to their friends. In 1996 they came to the attention of Zondervan Publishing, and in 1997 demand skyrocketed into a national phenomenon when legendary radio broadcaster Paul Harvey mentioned them on his syndicated radio program every day for a week. Soon Christians from coast to coast were asking *"What would Jesus do?"*

A Fly In The Theological Ointment

Charles Sheldon's theology had been shaped by forces other than the Scriptures, including what is now referred to as "Christian Socialism," and that involves a little history. In the late 18th and early 19th Centuries, Christianity had come under relentless and withering attacks by skeptics who questioned and denied the supernatural and miraculous aspects of Scripture, such things as miracles, the virgin birth, the deity of Christ, the bodily resurrection of Jesus, etc. If it was miraculous, they denied it. Christians, churches and

The Least Of These

denominations were slowly and relentlessly forced to take sides and to declare whether they affirmed the "historical Jesus" or the "miraculous Jesus."[13]

Unfortunately, when the miraculous and the supernatural aspects of the New Testament are removed, Jesus is no longer a divine savior but merely a religious teacher, a moral example and a doer of good deeds. Charles Sheldon stood in this stream of Christianity. For Sheldon, the role of the Church was not to offer a divine savior and supernatural redemption. Rather, the role of the Church was to offer a superior moral example - embodied in the person of Jesus - and to work to improve the conditions of life in this world. Sheldon's approach to the Christian life was expressed in the phrase, *"What Would Jesus Do?,"* with Jesus being a superior moral example rather than a divine Saviour figure. Sheldon's book and ideas had a profound impact upon other "Christian Socialists" such as Harry Emerson Fosdick and Walter Rauschenbusch, who would become one of the most articulate theologians and proponents of the "Social Gospel."[14] Rauschenbush acknowledged that his own Social Gospel owed its inspiration directly to Sheldon's novel.

The "social gospel" of Sheldon, Rauschenbusch and those who would follow them emphasized good deeds devoid of

---

[13]Albert Schweitzer, *The Quest of the Historical Jesus: A Critical Study of its Progress from Reimarus to Wrede*, Translated by W. Montgomery, First English Edition, (Great Britain: A & C Black, 1910). More recent versions of this school of thought have included "The Jesus Project" and the "Jesus Seminar."

[14]See Walter A. Rauschenbusch, *A Theology for the Social Gospel* (New York: Abingdon Press, 1917).

Whatever Happened To Incarnational Truth?

any miraculous Kingdom message of sin, personal redemption and salvation. Good deeds became an end-in-themselves, the expression of a superior moral example modeled after Jesus. And "salvation" was re-defined and reduced to the elimination of social ills (hunger, poverty, sickness, etc.) in this life.

The theological liberalism of Sheldon, Rauschenbush and others alienated the Evangelical Christian community of the early 20th Century (generally referred to as "Fundamentalists") and brought about a two-fold reaction. The first reaction was a positive one in that it forced the Evangelical Christian community to re-state and re-emphasize the importance of historic Orthodox Christian doctrine.[15] But the second reaction was very unfortunate and has had lasting repercussions. The Evangelical Christian community reacted by identifying the idea of "good deeds" with the Social Gospel and theological liberalism. We stopped asking *"What would Jesus do?"* because both the question and the answers had become "tainted." As a result, Evangelicals came to minimize the importance of good deeds in favor of emphasizing the importance theological purity, personal evangelism and missions. The ongoing result has been that for nearly 100 years Evangelical Christianity has lost the "salt and light" of good deeds and has reduced biblical faith to an intellectual assent to a set of correct

---

[15]Out of this "Fundamentalist-Modernist" controversy came a series of 90 essays entitled, *The Fundamentals: A Testimony To The Truth* (generally referred to simply as *The Fundamentals*) edited by A. C. Dixon and later by Reuben A. Torrey (successor to D.L. Moody). The 90 essays were written by 64 different authors and came to define "Fundamentalist" Christianity for decades to follow.

The Least Of These

doctrines expressed in a personal profession of faith. And more often than not, it represented a profession of faith devoid of any necessary relationship between personal faith and practical good deeds. [16]

So, when I refer to good deeds, or when we ask ourselves the question, *"What would Jesus do?"* I am not talking about the Social Gospel (and neither was Janie Tinklenberg

> *"We are asking what a Jesus-shaped spirituality looks like when lived out in the real world."*

when she urged her youth group to ask themselves *"What would Jesus do?"*). Quite the opposite! We are asking what a Jesus-shaped spirituality looks like when lived out in the real world. We are talking about the biblical gospel, consisting of a profession of genuine faith in a supernatural Savior which produces a Jesus-shaped spirituality encompassing BOTH right belief (correct doctrine) AND the visible fruit of good deeds.

A Gospel That Produces A Jesus-Shaped Spirituality

The genuine good news concerning the Kingdom of God produces disciples who are committed to pursuing a Jesus-shaped spirituality. And any genuine Jesus-shaped spirituality will express itself in two important dimensions, one vertical and one horizontal.

---

[16]The history and disastrous consequences of the withdrawal of Evangelical Christians from the social sphere has been explored by David O. Moberg in *The Great Reversal: Evangelism and Social Concern,* Lippincott: Revised edition (1977)

Whatever Happened To Incarnational Truth?

The good news of the Kingdom of God first manifests itself in the life of the individual who is confronted with the message of sin, repentance, forgiveness, redemption and faith. This produces what I call the *"vertical consequences"* of the good news of the Kingdom. It changes the individual's relationship with God, resulting in personal redemption and salvation, and creating a new vertical dimension to their spirituality. They now have a relationship with God that they did not posses before.

But the consequences of the good news of the Kingdom of God are also horizontal. The *"horizontal consequences"* are those which impact the world as the redeemed individual begins to pursue and express his (or her) Jesus-shaped spirituality through personal obedience to the biblical commands to engage in good deeds. In other words, it is the consequences of redeemed people pursuing a Jesus-shaped spirituality and asking themselves, *"What did Jesus do and teach concerning this situation, and what would He do if He were here today?"* These horizontal consequences become our public testimony - our "salt and light" - to those around us. This combination of both the vertical and the horizontal consequences of the message of the Kingdom of God are the practical fulfillment of Jesus' declaration to the Pharisees:

"And he said to him, 'You shall love the Lord your God with all your heart and with all your soul and with all your mind. (That's the "vertical" part) *This is the great and first commandment. And a second is like it: You shall love your neighbor as yourself.* (That's the "horizontal" part) *On these two commandments depend all the Law and the Prophets'."* (Matthew 22:37-40)

The Least Of These

You and I might disagree on many things, but could we agree on two points before we move on? *First,* could we agree that no one has ever loved God with all his heart, soul and mind more than Jesus did; and that no one has ever

> *". . . a Jesus-shaped spirituality will express its love for God and its love for our neighbors through what Scripture refers to as good deeds."*

loved his neighbor as himself more than Jesus did? Are we agreed? Good! *Second,* can we agree that, since Jesus is our example, any pursuit of a Jesus-shaped spirituality must involve BOTH loving God AND loving our neighbor? Finally, it is my contention that a Jesus-shaped spirituality will express its love for God and its love for our neighbors through what Scripture refers to as good deeds.

Faith, Good Deeds And Vacuum Cleaners

"What good is it, my brothers, if someone says he has faith but does not have works? Can that faith save him? If a brother or sister is poorly clothed and lacking in daily food, and one of you says to them, 'Go in peace, be warmed and filled,' without giving them the things needed for the body, what good is that? So also faith by itself, if it does not have works, is dead." (James 2:14-17)

The Apostle James understood the relationship between faith and good deeds (the Greek word for "works" used here is *ergon*, the same word used in all occurrences of the phrase

Whatever Happened To Incarnational Truth?

"good deeds"). James' message is consistent with the rest of New Testament teaching regarding good deeds. The New Testament consistently teaches that a genuine miraculous faith will produce a Jesus-shaped spirituality which

> *"Genuine faith produces fruit, including the fruit of good deeds. The absence of good deeds calls into question the genuineness of any professed faith."*

expresses itself in the genuine fruit of good deeds. That is James' point. Genuine faith produces fruit, including the fruit of good deeds. The absence of good deeds ("works") calls into question the genuineness of any professed "faith." Healthy trees produce fruit. When fruit is consistently absent, the health and viability of the tree must be questioned (Matthew 12:33). That's the biblical principle.

My experience among professing Christians in the Church over nearly four decades informs me that far too many Christians regard good deeds the same way a door-to-door vacuum cleaner salesman regards the home demonstration of his latest vacuum cleaner. No vacuum cleaner salesman really wants to come back to the same home week after week and vacuum the same carpet for the same person who can't decide whether or not to purchase the salesman's latest cleaner. No. The salesman hopes that a quick demonstration of his machine's superior cleaning ability will result in a spontaneous and immediate decision to buy.

So it is with most of our good deeds. We hope (indeed, we expect) that the performance of a quick good deed - the spiritual equivalent of a vacuum "demo" - will result in an immediate decision to "buy." And when that quick decision is not forthcoming we lose interest and move on, leaving bewildered unbelievers wondering what that little episode was all about . . . and whether Christians really care about them at all. It's time to ask ourselves a hard question. Is that what Jesus would do? Is that what He did - offer His love, compassion and healing like a cheap vacuum demo in the hope that his audience would "buy"?

Miracles And the Plow of Good Deeds

Engaging in good deeds on a consistent basis can be compared with plowing fallow ground (i.e., ground that has lain dormant and unplowed). Plowing fallow ground outside the comfortable four walls of our churches (and, yes, that includes house churches) is hard work - more work than a quick vacuum cleaner demo! I believe Scripture acknowledges the challenge of plowing fallow ground with good deeds by emphasizing the importance of good deeds over 30 times in the New Testament. The Holy Spirit knew we would need regular, consistent encouragement to keep going.

Author A. W. Tozer also expressed this reality - the challenge of plowing fallow ground - when he wrote his wonderful article entitled *"Miracles Follow The Plow."* [17] Tozer argued that if we truly want to see God move in miraculous power in the Church today, then we need to get out of our comfortable

---

[17]A.W. Tozer, *"Miracles Follow The Plow"* excerpted in Warren Wiersbe, **The Best of A.W. Tozer** (Camphill: Christian Publications, 1992) Copyright Baker Book House Company 1978, page 243

Whatever Happened To Incarnational Truth?

boxes and go plow some fallow ground,

"The only way to power for such a church is to come out of hiding and once more take the danger-encircled path of obedience. Its security is its deadliest foe. The church that fears the plow writes its own epitaph: the church that uses the plow walks in the way of revival."

Tozer's meaning is simple. If you and I want to see God multiply food it probably won't happen in the fellowship hall at the Church potluck. More often than not, miracles follow the plow of our good deeds. Just ask Jeff.

Jeff was an unbeliever who lived in the upstairs apartment at the original Off Broadway ministry location in the West Central neighborhood of Spokane (See Chapter 8). He occasionally helped out with preparing food for the Thursday night neighborhood gathering (it later moved to Monday nights). After one particular gathering Larry Whiston - an elder in the Off Broadway fellowship - found Jeff sitting on the steps around 2:00AM with a very serious look on his face.
"I cooked the food tonight, Larry," Jeff said very emphatically.
"Yeah, I know," Larry replied.
"You don't understand. I cooked the food tonight," Jeff said again, this time visibly shaken.
"Yeah, I know. What's your point, Jeff."
Then came the reply.
"We fed more people than I had food to cook for them," Jeff said with tears in his eyes. According to this shaken unbeliever who had prepared the evening meal, God had multiplied food that night, and he had witnessed it. Jeff made a profession of faith shortly after that experience.

The Least Of These

Miracles, you see, most often follow the plow of "good deeds," the manifestation of a Jesus-shaped spirituality. And that is where we now want to turn our attention.

Reflections For A Jesus-Shaped Spirituality

Reflection Question #1 - What have you learned about incarnational truth and a Jesus-shaped spirituality that you did not know before?

Reflection Question #2 - Discuss the difference between "attractional" Christianity and "incarnational" Christianity.

Reflection Question #3 - When was the last time you asked yourself, *"What would Jesus do?"* as you made a major decision?

Reflection Question #4 - What is the difference between biblical good deeds and "the social gospel"?

Reflection Question #5 - Discuss good deeds you have done or been involved with to break up fallow ground and to plant seed for the Kingdom of God in the life of someone else?

Chapter 3

A Jesus-Shaped Spirituality

"You yourselves know what happened throughout all Judea, beginning from Galilee after the baptism that John proclaimed: how God anointed Jesus of Nazareth with the Holy Spirit and with power. He went about doing good and healing all who were oppressed by the devil, for God was with him." (Acts 10:38)

Who Shapes Your Spirituality?[18]

If we are going to pursue good deeds as an integral part of a Jesus-shaped spirituality, then we need to ask ourselves if the whole concept of "doing good" was part of Jesus' own spirituality while here on earth. I think the Apostle Peter gives us the answer to this question in Acts 10. In that passage Peter summarizes the life, times and ministry of Jesus for a gathering of Gentiles in the home of Cornelius, a Roman Centurion. Peter describes how Jesus *"went about doing good and healing all who were oppressed by the devil."* The Greek verb translated "doing good" (*euergeteo*) is the same root stem as *ergon*, "deed," (the prefix *eu* meaning "good" has been added). According to Peter's summation of Jesus' activities, Jesus went about Palestine *"doing good (deeds)."*

---

[18]We examine the development of a Jesus-shaped spirituality within the context of biblical discipleship in our book *And They Dreamt Of A Kingdom*, available on our website from Amazon.com. .

The Least Of These

My friend Wolfgang Simson likes to say that Jesus basically did three things. He invited himself over for dinner at other people's homes, He told stories about the Kingdom of God and He cast out demons. Hmmm, not bad work if you can get it! But, if Peter is correct that Jesus went about "doing good," it's a fair question to ask about the nature of those good deeds. What exactly did Jesus do?

Now, before we look at how Jesus *"did good"* to specific groups of people we need to look at His basic attitude toward serving people in general. Jesus tells us exactly what He thinks in Luke Chapter 6:

"If you love those who love you, what benefit is that to you? For even sinners love those who love them. And if you do good to those who do good to you, what benefit is that to you? For even sinners do the same. And if you lend to those from whom you expect to receive, what credit is that to you? Even sinners lend to sinners, to get back the same amount. But love your enemies, and do good, and lend, expecting nothing in return, and your reward will be great, and you will be sons of the Most High, for he is kind to the ungrateful and the evil. Be merciful, even as your Father is merciful." (Luke 6:32-36)

Some Christians want to argue that the biblical commands to engage in good deeds are intended for Christians and how they should treat fellow believers. I think that

> *"Jesus Himself never limited His good deeds to those who believed in Him."*

Christians are certainly included in such instructions. But it

A Jesus-Shaped Spirituality

should be clear from this passage in Luke that Jesus Himself never limited His good deeds to those who believed in Him. In fact, His point here is that even "sinners" take care of their own, but His followers are to be different. They are to do good to their enemies, just as God Himself *"is kind to ungrateful and evil men."* According to Jesus, we - through our good deeds - are to show others the same mercy God has shown us. O.K., now we're ready to take a look at how Jesus *"did good"* to specific groups of people.

Jesus Befriended the Marginalized. There were many marginalized groups in 1st Century Palestine, people whom the religion-shaped spirituality of institutional Judaism either pushed to the margins of Jewish social and religious life or regarded as "unclean" under the Old Testament ceremonial laws. We only have time and space here to talk about a few of them.

1. Gentiles - Simply put, a Gentile (Greek: _ethnos_) was anyone who was not a Jew. Peter summed up the situation well in Acts 10:28 when he spoke to the Gentiles gathered in the home of Cornelius, *"And he said to them, 'You yourselves know how unlawful it is for a Jew to associate with or to visit anyone of another nation, but God has shown me that I should not call any person common or unclean'."*

As a good Jew, Peter had grown up with religious Judaism's *"rules of exclusion"* which had turned the 612 commandments of the Law into over 5,000 religious laws which now governed the religion-shaped spirituality of every obedient Jew. Was it really unlawful for a Jewish man *"to associate with a foreigner or to visit him"*? Not according to the Law of Moses. Rather, this exclusionary idea was a prohibition which had been added by religious Judaism and had been given the force of law by the religious authorities. Such religious exclusions had created many "marginalized" groups.

> *"Jesus went out of His way to associate with those marginalized people in order to 'do good' and to touch them with the Kingdom of God."*

And Jesus went out of His way to associate with those marginalized people in order to "do good" and to touch them with the Kingdom of God.

2. Women - The 1st Century Jewish attitude toward women placed them in an inferior position to men. A Jewish morning prayer declared, *"You are blessed, O God, for You did not make me a Woman."* But Jesus ignored such religious conventions and included numerous women among His followers, some of whom supported Him out of their financial resources (see Luke 8:1-3).[19]

3. Samaritans - Between Jerusalem and Galilee lay the land of Samaria. The Jews of Jerusalem and Judea regarded Samaritans as "half-breeds," products of interbreeding between the Jewish remnant and the Assyrians, Babylonians and other locals. They practiced their own form of Judaism and the rivalry between the Samaritans and the Jews was

---

[19]For a more in-depth look at how Jesus reached out to marginalized women, see Lessons 14 and 35 in our book, ***And They Dreamt Of A Kingdom***, available on our website from Amazon.com.

intense. A good Jew would not speak to a Samaritan and would go out of his way to avoid one. When it came to making the trip from Jerusalem to Galilee most Jews would take the long way around by crossing over east of the Jordan River in order to avoid passing through Samaria. To minister directly to a Samaritan woman (John 4) was a flagrant violation of Jewish social protocol. To use a Samaritan as an example of what it meant to be a good neighbor (see Luke 10:33 and the parable of the *"Good Samaritan"*) would shock a Jewish audience. To call a fellow Jew a "Samaritan" (which the religious leaders did to Jesus in John 8:48) was a slur and an insult. And yet Jesus intentionally reached out to Samaritans on more than one occasion (see Luke 17:11-19) as He embraced the marginalized of Israel.

4. Lepers - If you've ever seen the movie "Ben-Hur" then you have a pretty good idea of the 1st Century Jewish attitude toward leprosy. They were ostracized from the life of God's people and forced to live alone or in leper colonies. In all the history of Israel there was no record of any Jew ever being healed of leprosy according to the procedures set forth in the Mosaic Law (see Leviticus 13). Leprosy was a life sentence of ritual and religious uncleanness, and personal separation and isolation from the community. But Jesus broke all religious and social conventions with respect to lepers. Although He could have healed them with a word, he made it a point to "do good" by touching them (Matthew 8:2). For Jesus, it wasn't enough to "do good" by healing lepers with a touch. It was important for Jesus to validate their new status by dining in their home (Mark 14:3), something no good Jewish religious leader would EVER do.

The Least Of These

5. Tax collectors And Sinners - It was a frequent accusation leveled by religious leaders and directed at Jesus that he spent way too much time hanging out with *"tax-gatherers and sinners."* Here's one example:

"And it happened that as He was reclining at the table in the house, behold many tax-gatherers and sinners came and were dining with Jesus and His disciples. And when the Pharisees saw this, they said to His disciples, 'Why is your Teacher eating with the tax-gatherers and sinners?' But when He heard this, He said, 'It is not those who are healthy who need a physician, but those who are sick. But go and learn what this means, 'I DESIRE COMPASSION, AND NOT SACRIFICE,' for I did not come to call the righteous, but sinners." (Matthew 9:10-13) [20]

In 1st Century Palestine tax collectors were particularly odious because they were frequently Jews under public contract to the Romans to collect taxes from their fellow Jews on behalf of Rome. As a result

> *"Throughout His earthly ministry Jesus intentionally reached out to 'do good' to the most marginalized people in all of Palestine.*

they were marginalized and treated as worse than Gentiles. In the thinking of 1st Century Judaism there was no moral difference between a "sinner" and a "tax-collector." Both were to be avoided and shunned by all good religious Jews (which explains a lot about the story of Zaacheus in Luke 19). Jesus

---

[20]See also Matthew 11:19; Mark 2:15-16; Luke 5:30; 6:32-33; 7:34-37; 15:1-7; 19:7

A Jesus-Shaped Spirituality

embraced such marginalized people. He not only invited Himself to dinner in their homes (see Luke 19:5), he called such people to be His disciples (see Levi in Luke 5:27).

Throughout His earthly ministry Jesus intentionally reached out to "do good" to the most marginalized people in all of Palestine. Gentiles. Women. Samaritans. Lepers. Tax collectors. And a wide assortment of "sinners." Simply stated, Jesus loved the marginalized, and He taught His disciples to love them, too.

". . . contrary to religious opinions both then and now, the mission of God in this world continues to be the calling of sinners, not the righteous, to repentance."

Not much has changed in 2,000 years. Religious people today continue to believe that we should spend most of our ministry time preaching to and teaching the choir, while limiting our good deeds to helping fellow believers, rather than hanging out with unbelievers. But contrary to religious opinions both then and now, the mission of God in this world continues to be the calling of sinners, not the righteous, to repentance. And that requires us to "do good" to unbelievers and the marginalized outside the four walls of the Church - including house church. But at an even deeper level it forces us to ask ourselves who "the marginalized" of our own day might be. You can't "do

"You can't do good for people in need if you can't even identify them."

good" for people in need if you can't even identify them.

Jesus demonstrated personal compassion toward those in need. Compassion has always been one of God's eternal attributes. In the Old Testament the Hebrew root (*racham*) expressing God's compassion, pity or mercy occurs some 90 times. In the New Testament the Greek word expressing the compassion of Jesus (*splagchnizomai*) occurs some 20 times. Both words communicate such a "visceral" or "gut" response to the needs of those in distress that the older translators used such phrases as *"bowels of compassion"* to express the intensity of these words (see the KJV rendering of Genesis 43:30, *"and his bowels did yearn"* or Philippians 1:8, *"how greatly I long after you all in the bowels of Jesus Christ"*).

"And Jesus went throughout all the cities and villages, teaching in their synagogues and proclaiming the gospel of the kingdom and healing every disease and every affliction. When he saw the crowds, he had compassion for them, because they were harassed and helpless, like sheep without a shepherd. Then he said to his disciples, 'The harvest is plentiful, but the laborers are few; therefore pray earnestly to the Lord of the harvest to send out laborers into his harvest'."(Matthew 9:35-38)

This passage tells us that Jesus' itinerant ministry was widespread throughout Palestine and involved four activities. The first three are seen in verse 35: teaching, proclaiming and healing. The fourth activity is easy to miss. Greek likes to use participles to describe the ongoing circumstances surrounding the action of the primary verb. These are called

A Jesus-Shaped Spirituality

"circumstantial participles." In verse 36 the circumstantial participle is *"seeing,"* which sets the stage for the primary verb, *"He felt compassion."* Jesus taught. Jesus

> *"It is difficult, if not impossible, to have compassion on people we can't even see."*

proclaimed. Jesus healed. But Jesus also "saw." He saw the immediate distress of the human condition and was moved with compassion.

What comes next is interesting. In verses 37 and 38 Jesus makes a now-famous declaration, *"On the one hand, the harvest is plentiful, while on the other hand the laborers are few."* Jesus then urges the disciples to "beg" the Lord of the harvest to send additional laborers into his harvest. Now, this passage raises an important question: *"What are these laborers supposed to do in the harvest?"* Based upon the context, they are to do what Jesus did. Obviously they are to teach, to proclaim and to heal. But they are also to SEE the human condition and to be moved with compassion. It is difficult, if not impossible, to have compassion on people we can't even see.

The compassion of Jesus was personal and practical. He understood that some people needed to hear the proclamation of the Kingdom. He knew that others needed healing. He knew that still others needed demonic deliverance. And he knew that others needed to be fed. We see this expressed in Matthew 15. There Jesus

> *"The compassion of Jesus was personal and practical."*

ministers to multitudes of people who are following Him. Some are taught. Some are healed. Others experience demonic deliverance. But after three days of non-stop ministry, the multitude is exhausted and hungry. Jesus sees it, and is moved with *compassion* (the same

"Those of us seeking a Jesus-shaped spirituality must recover a Jesus-shaped compassion which sees the human condition and is moved to do something about it."

compassion expressed in Matthew 9:35-38):

"Then Jesus called his disciples to him and said, 'I have compassion (<u>splagchnizomai</u>) on the crowd because they have been with me now three days and have nothing to eat. And I am unwilling to send them away hungry, lest they faint on the way'." (Matthew 15:32)

Again, the compassion of Jesus was both personal and practical, and expressed itself in good deeds toward those in need. When people were hungry, Jesus saw, He understood, and He fed them. Those of us seeking a Jesus-shaped spirituality must recover a Jesus-shaped compassion which sees the human condition and is moved to do something about it.

Jesus emphasized personal ministry to "the least of these." If you and I still need a summary of Jesus' attitude regarding the importance of doing good with respect to the marginalized people of this world, we will find that summary expressed in Jesus' own words in Matthew, Chapter 25:

A Jesus-Shaped Spirituality

"Then the King will say to those on his right, 'Come, you who are blessed by my Father, inherit the kingdom prepared for you from the foundation of the world. For I was hungry and you gave me food, I was thirsty and you gave me drink, I was a stranger and you welcomed me, I was naked and you clothed me, I was sick and you visited me, I was in prison and you came to me.' Then the righteous will answer him, saying, 'Lord, when did we see you hungry and feed you, or thirsty and give you drink? And when did we see you a stranger and welcome you, or naked and clothe you? And when did we see you sick or in prison and visit you?' And the King will answer them, 'Truly, I say to you, as you did it to one of the least of these my brothers, you did it to me'." (Matthew 25:34-40)

We will treat this passage in more detail later in Chapter 5, but for now I want to simply note that Jesus offers us a list of marginalized "people groups" who constitute *"the least of these."* Is this list exhaustive, or even final? No. I don't think so. But it does offer us a starting place, along with insight into the heart of God. But it also includes a clear warning to us that God will hold us accountable on Judgment Day for how we responded to *"the least of these."* And that alone should be enough to get our attention, and to provoke us to greater love and good deeds! Any pursuit of a Jesus-shaped spirituality must pass through Matthew 25:41ff. So, who are these marginalized people? They include:

    1) The hungry,
    2) The thirsty,
    3) The stranger,
    4) The naked,
    5) The sick,

The Least Of These

6) The prisoner.

Is this "all"? Probably not, but it's a good place to start.

Reflections For A Jesus-Shaped Spirituality

Reflection Question #1 - What have you learned about a Jesus-shaped spirituality that you did not know before?

Reflection Question #2 - What have you learned about how Jesus loved and reached out to marginalized people, and how could that change the way you view the importance of good deeds in your life and ministry?

Reflection Question #3 - Who are the marginalized people in your life or sphere of influence? Use the box-chart on the following page to make a "think list" of marginalized people in your sphere of influence, such as: unemployed friends, racial minorities, the working poor, strangers (such as illegal immigrants?), the homeless (like homeless teens in your child's school district), unwed moms, women fleeing domestic violence or the sex trade, ex-felons seeking employment, and others. Beside each name write something you could do for that individual to show the personal and practical compassion of Christ toward them.

A Jesus-Shaped Spirituality

My Think List For "The Least of These"	
Person/Group	*Good Deed Idea*

The Least Of These

Chapter 4

What Do The Scriptures Say?

So far we have looked at the idea of incarnational ministry as opposed to attractional ministry, and the need for a conscious movement into what we are referring to as a Jesus-shaped spirituality. We also looked at the question *"What would Jesus do?"* and made a distinction between biblical good deeds and the concept of "the social gospel." We then looked at the life of Jesus and saw that a Jesus-shaped spirituality must include the concept of doing good, particularly to the marginalized and to *"the least of these."* Now we want to take a closer look at the overall teaching of the New Testament concerning the concept of good deeds. Our goal is to better understand what role they are supposed to play in the Jesus-shaped spirituality of the individual believer as well as in the life of the organic church, including the one which meets in your house.

It may come as a surprise to you (frankly, it did to me) that the New Testament has a great deal to say about the importance of good deeds. And that's where we need to start our discussion. The concept of good deeds or good works occurs some 32 times in the New Testament. Our English words "works" and "deeds" are simply two alternate translations of the same Greek word, *ergon*. For the sake of consistency we are rendering *ergon* as "deeds." Those 32 occurrences are almost equally divided between two Greek phrases (*agathos ergon* and *kalos ergon*), which are so similar in use and meaning as to be interchangeable. Paul uses them interchangeably in 1 Timothy 5:10. The word *agathos* suggests something that is intrinsically good, whereas *kalos* describes something

> *". . . the New Testament has a great deal to say about the importance of good deeds."*

which, in addition to being intrinsically good, is also outwardly attractive, pleasing or useful. The idea is simple: the intrinsically good work which God has begun in the life of every true believer finds its outward expression in the fruit of apparent, attractive and useful good deeds. And when the visible, useful fruit of good deeds is absent from the life of a professing believer, it calls into question whether or not God has actually begun any intrinsically good work in his or her life. Good trees produce good fruit. That's the biblical principle (Matthew 3:10; 7:17-19; 12:33). Where there is no fruit, the viability of the tree must be questioned.

In order to more fully appreciate what the New Testament has to say about the whole idea of good deeds we will look at some of the most critical Scripture passages on the subject. From these passages I want to draw some *"Good Deeds Principles"* - basic statements which

> *". . . the intrinsically good work which God has begun in the life of every true believer finds its outward expression in the fruit of apparent, attractive and useful good deeds."*

summarize the role of good deeds in the life of any disciple seeking a Jesus-shaped spirituality. So, let's get started.

What Do The Scriptures Say?

Good Deeds Principle # 1: Our Works Are Our Witness

"But the testimony that I have is greater than that of John. For the works that the Father has given me to accomplish, the very works that I am doing, bear witness about me that the Father has sent me." (John 5:36)

The most appropriate place to begin our understanding of good works is with Jesus Himself. Jesus was constantly being confronted with the same question by the unbelieving religious leadership of His day: *"How do we know that you are who and what you say you are?"* (See John 2:18; 6:30) On this particular occasion in the fifth chapter of John's gospel Jesus offers His skeptics two reasons why they should believe Him. *First,* He argues that they have the witness of John the Baptist, whom the people and many of the religious leaders regarded as a prophet. But Jesus offers his skeptics a *second*, simple answer to their question: *"Look at my deeds,"* he says. *"My deeds speak for themselves."*

This is a bold statement, so bold that it would be easy to conclude that Jesus is establishing some new principle here. But the reality is that He is simply restating an existing truth: we are known by our fruit. We can state this principle in the same terms that Jesus did here by saying, *"Our works are our witness."* Just as the works of Jesus bore witness to the reality that He came from God, so, too, our works bear witness that God is our Father and that Jesus is our Lord. As we will soon see, just as the Father gave Jesus works to accomplish, so God has appointed good works for every believer to walk in. And our willingness to walk in those good deeds will bear public witness to the private reality of our

The Least Of These

Jesus-shaped spirituality.

Good Deeds Principle # 2: Be A Light

"You are the light of the world. A city set on a hill cannot be hidden. Nor do people light a lamp and put it under a basket, but on a stand, and it gives light to all in the house. In the same way, let your light shine before others, so that they may see your good works and give glory to your Father who is in heaven." (Matthew 5:14-16)

Ask yourself a simple question: *"What does it mean for me to be the light of the world?"* An insightful author once asked a challenging question, *"If a can opener won't open any cans, is it really a can opener?"* Just because a certain tool is called a can opener and just because it happens to look like other can openers we have known or used, is it still a can opener if it won't open any cans?

Let's apply this to Jesus' parable. . . and to our lives. When is a lamp no longer a lamp? When it no longer does what lamps are suppose to do, namely, give light. Jesus says that you and I are the light of the world. He doesn't say that you and I *could* be the light of the world or *should* be the light of the world or *will* be the light of the world. No. He says that you and I *ARE* the light of the world. And what does a light do? It shines and *"gives light to all who are in the house."* At this point the natural question for you and me should be, *"How do we do this? How do we let our light shine before men?"*

Fortunately, Jesus gives us the answer: Through our good deeds. Simply stated, our good deeds are the vehicle

What Do The Scriptures Say?

through which the light of our Jesus-shaped spirituality shines before men in such a way that they see our good deeds and glorify God as a result. And the Greek word for men here (*anthropos*) is the word for men in general, "mankind" (as opposed to a much more limited audience such as "the church").

Let's be clear on this point, as there seems to be much confusion in the Church regarding it. Our good deeds make us a light to an unbelieving world. Some Christians want to argue that the good deeds talked about in the New Testament are to be done primarily (if not exclusively) by Christians for other Christians. Proponents of this view argue that unbelievers will see how much we love one another through our good deeds toward one another and will be so impressed that they will glorify God and believe. I have three basic responses to this argument.

My **first** response is a question: *"How's it working for you?"* If this interpretation is true, then our lives as believers should be filled with good deeds toward one another, and unbelievers should be coming to our Churches in droves because of how much we love one another! Unfortunately, proponents of this view fail to live up to their own restrictive interpretation of this passage. That doesn't mean it is wrong, but it does mean we are terribly inconsistent!

Second, on a practical level, I do not believe it is possible to *"let your light so shine before men"* by sitting in a Church building for two or three hours a week while the rest of the unbelieving world is out doing other things. Our Postmodern western culture is going to considerable lengths to avoid us.

The Least Of These

The vast majority of unbelievers simply aren't attracted to our elaborate buildings and programs, not even to the EPIC ones. Overall church attendance has fallen dramatically, from 42% of adults in 1965 to as low as 20% today. The attractional model of church simply isn't working anymore. The masses simply aren't beating a path to the doors of our attractional churches to see our good deeds or to hear our message f the Kingdom.

But my *third* response is more to the biblical point. I do not believe Scripture obviously or necessarily teaches a restrictive scope or our good deeds, either here in Matthew 5 or in any other passage. Should believers express their love for one another through good deeds done for fellow believers. Of course we should. But is that the limit for the biblical commands concerning good deeds? Not according to Jesus, as we read earlier in Luke 6:32-36 where Jesus specifically commanded us to love our enemies and to "do good" to them (see verse 35).

In addition, in Matthew 5 Jesus declares that we believers are the light of the world (_kosmos_), and I don't know about you, but "the world" sounds a lot bigger than the four walls of any church. Jesus seems to be laying down a basic principle: believers seeking to live out a Jesus-shaped spirituality have an obligation to shine the light of their good deeds in such a way that the people of this world (_anthropos_ - "mankind") will see those good deeds and respond by glorifying God. After all, isn't that what Jesus did?

In a curious historical note, the early Church historian Eusebius states that story of Jesus' life, death, resurrection

What Do The Scriptures Say?

and ascension - His life story including His good deeds - were communicated by Pontius Pilate to the Roman Emperor Tiberius who further presented the report to the Roman Senate.[21] Perhaps this is why Paul could say to King Festus in Acts 26:25-26,

"I am not out of my mind, most excellent Festus, but I am speaking true and rational words. For the king knows about these things, and to him I speak boldly. For I am persuaded that none of these things has escaped his notice, for this has not been done in a corner."

In other words (Maurice's interpretation) Jesus' life and good deeds had become legendary. The light of His life, including His good deeds, had shown in the darkness, not only throughout Palestine but all the way to Rome and its leaders.

Finally, have you ever wondered how Jesus' teaching on this issue affected His own disciples? I think Jesus' words here in Matthew 5 had a profound impact on at least one of His disciples: Simon Peter. Why? Because Peter refers to them years later in 1 Peter,

"Beloved, I urge you as sojourners and exiles to abstain from the passions of the flesh, which wage war against your soul. Keep your conduct among the Gentiles honorable, so that when they speak against you as evildoers, they may see your good deeds and glorify God on the day of visitation." (1 Peter 2:11-12)

---

[21]See Eusebius' **Church History**, Book 2, Section 2. Eusebius quotes Tertullian who relates this story in full.

The Least Of These

Did you catch it there at the end of verse 12? Peter tells his readers that, through their excellent behavior _among the Gentiles_, unbelievers will see their good deeds and will glorify God. Peter got the point. Do we?

Good Deeds Principle #3: Find Your Purpose

"For by grace you have been saved through faith. And this is not your own doing; it is the gift of God, not a result of works, so that no one may boast. For we are his workmanship, created in Christ Jesus for good works, which God prepared beforehand, that we should walk in them." (Ephesians 2:8-10)

If you haven't read or seen a copy of Rick Warren's mega-best seller, **_The Purpose Driven Life_** then you've either been living on Mars or some place genuinely out of touch with reality - like inside the

". . . millions of professing Christians lack biblical purpose in their spiritual lives. The question is, 'Why?'"

Washington, D.C. beltway. Now, 30 million copies later the Christian community (who bought most of those books) finally knows that God has a purpose for their lives. This mega-selling phenomenon bears sad testimony to a disturbing reality: millions of professing Christians lack biblical purpose in their spiritual lives. The question is, _"Why?"_

I want to suggest two possible reasons for this lack of purpose among professing believers. **_First,_** I believe one

What Do The Scriptures Say?

reason for this lack of purpose among professing Christians is widespread bad teaching about salvation itself. The above passage from Ephesians clearly teaches that biblical salvation is by God's grace working through faith, and that all three components (the salvation, the grace and the faith) are all free gifts from God. They cannot be earned through works of any kind, so that no can boast of having earned his or her salvation. God freely gives, and we freely receive.

But there is a downside to how this marvelous truth has been communicated. Far too many professing believers have been taught to view their salvation as an end to be achieved - a destination to be arrived at - rather than viewing it for what it really is, the beginning of a purpose filled journey into a Jesus-shaped spirituality of faith expressed through good deeds. Too many professing Christians have been "saved to be saved" (or at least "saved to attend church"). Once the destination of personal salvation has been achieved they can move on with the more important things - like watching *Dancing With The Stars*!

The **second** reason for this lack of purpose among professing believers has to do with the fact that all too often we teach the first half of this passage from

> *"A Jesus-shaped spirituality is a spirituality with a purpose."*

Ephesians Chapter 2 (the whole *"saved by grace through faith"* part) while ignoring the second half. According to the second half of this passage, we have been saved *FOR* a divinely appointed purpose.[22] We have been created in Christ Jesus *"for the purpose"* of walking in those good works which God Himself has pre-prepared for each us. A Jesus-shaped spirituality is a spirituality with a purpose.

Let's restate this as follows: You and I will never discover or fulfill the purpose for which God called and saved us if we do not discover and walk in those good deeds which He has prepared for us. The lifelong challenge

"The fruit of good deeds in our life signifies that we are genuine followers of Jesus, rather than just occasional fans."

confronting every follower of Jesus is to discover those good deeds which God has already prepared for them to walk in. This is important. The fruit of good deeds in our life signifies that we are genuine followers of Jesus, rather than just occasional fans.

Good Deeds Principle #4: Learn To Overflow!

"Each one must give as he has decided in his heart, not reluctantly or under compulsion, for God loves a cheerful giver. And God is able to make all grace abound to you, so that having all sufficiency in all things at all times, you may abound in every good work. As it is written, 'He has distributed freely, he has given to the poor; his righteousness endures forever'." (2 Corinthians 9:7-9)

---

[22] The force of the Greek text in verse 10 is clearly a purpose clause, introduced with the preposition *hina*.

What Do The Scriptures Say?

Christian author A.W. Tozer once made the following observation:

"Christian theology teaches the doctrine of prevenient grace, which briefly stated means this, that before a man can seek God, God must first have sought the man." [23]

In other words, God is always first. His grace is always prevenient. It is always God who initiates, and we respond. In the Kingdom of God, in the matter of giving, this means that we do not "give-to-get" (despite a generation of "prosperity gospel" teaching to the contrary). Rather, it means that we give because we have received. God owes no man anything. Man owes God everything. The difference between these two perspectives is profound.

> *"We give to others because God has given to us. Our act of giving is an act of worship back to God for His goodness toward us."*

Scripture teaches that there is a "divine reciprocity" in God's dealings of grace toward His people. We give to others because God has given to us. Our act of giving is an act of worship back to God for His goodness toward us. But even that reciprocity begins with God, not with us. As believers we are the recipients of God's abounding, overflowing grace in our lives. Every believer should declare with David, *"my cup*

---

[23]A W. Tozer, **The Pursuit of God** (Harrisburg, PA: Christian Publications, Inc., 1948), page 11.

overflows" (Psalm 23: 5).[24] But it overflows with a divine purpose in mind, namely, so that we can overflow in every good deed toward others.

This is Jesus' point in Matthew 18:23-35 where Jesus tells a parable about a King who forgives the unpayable debt of his slave. But the slave, in turn, refuses to forgive his fellow slave for a much smaller debt. He failed to overflow with the very grace he had been shown. From a practical perspective, the more we experience and understand God's abundant grace toward us, the more we should be motivated to abound and overflow in those good works (particularly toward *"the poor"*) which God has prepared for us and which will cause men to glorify God.

We see a practical example of this type of "overflowing" good works in Acts 9:36ff,

"Now in Joppa there was a certain disciple named Tabitha (which translated in Greek is called Dorcas); this woman was abounding with deeds of kindness and charity, which she continually did."

We are told that Tabitha was *"abounding with deeds of kindness and charity* (literally, *"good deeds and alms-giving,"* i.e., to the poor)." Apparently she was well known for making articles of clothing and giving them away to the poor. In other words, she was one of those people who "overflowed" in good deeds, and everyone in Joppa knew it! The abundance

---

[24]The word "abound" in this passage is the Greek word *perisseuo* which describes *"something which comes in abundance, or overflows"* (Thayer).

of her good deeds toward others reflected the abundance of God's grace in her life. And even in death, God wasn't yet done with her good deeds. As a result of her good deeds to many people, when she died, all those whom she had helped came to weep and mourn,

> *"Never underestimate God's ability to use the obedience of your Jesus-shaped spirituality expressed through good deeds to display His power and to spread the gospel!"*

and to pay their respects. Many of them were probably unbelievers who had been touched by her life. And God had a surprise in store! They ALL became witnesses to God's power to raise the dead!

Never underestimate God's ability to use the obedience of your Jesus-shaped spirituality expressed through good deeds to display His power and to spread the gospel! He often uses our good deeds in ways we NEVER could have anticipated when we chose to obey. God is far more creative than the average Bible teacher who might want to minimize the importance of good deeds in your Christian walk.

Good Deeds Principle #5: Judgment Day Is Coming

"But because of your hard and impenitent heart you are storing up wrath for yourself on the day of wrath when God's righteous judgment will be revealed. He will RENDER TO EACH ONE ACCORDING TO HIS WORKS: to those who by patience in well-doing seek for glory and honor and immortality, he will give eternal life; but for those who are self-seeking and do not obey the truth, but obey

The Least Of These

unrighteousness, there will be wrath and fury. There will be tribulation and distress for every human being who does evil, the Jew first and also the Greek, but glory and honor and peace for everyone who does good, the Jew first and also the Greek." (Romans 2:5-10)

Let's begin with a question: *"What do you think is going to happen to you on the Day of Judgment?"* I am convinced that far too many professing Christians are in for a rude awakening on the Day of Judgment. Their expectation is something like this. They will arrive at the entrance to heaven and be asked to

". . . the New Testament also makes it equally clear that, in some way which you and I don't fully understand or appreciate, we will be judged and rewarded by the Lord for our deeds, whether good or bad."

present their church membership card, stamped with the date they "accepted Jesus" (date of baptism optional). The name and date on the card will be cross-referenced with the name and date recorded in a big book. Once their membership has been confirmed, the turnstile will open and they will be allowed to enter. Not so for the next poor schlub in line behind them who can't seem to find his membership card (thought I had it right here between my Sam's Club and my Costco cards).

O.K., I admit that this scenario is both fictional and a little exaggerated, but there is a grain of truth here. As Christians we believe that we are justified on the basis of our faith as evidenced when we "accepted Jesus" (for me it happened on Sunday, June 6, 1971). But do we also believe that we will

What Do The Scriptures Say?

one day be rewarded - given our workman's wage - for our deeds toward others, whether good or evil?

In addition to the clear biblical teaching concerning salvation freely given (see our discussion of Ephesians 2 under *"Good Deeds Principle #3"* above), the New Testament also makes it equally clear that, in some way which you and I don't fully understand or appreciate, we will be judged and rewarded by the Lord for our deeds, whether good or bad.

Now, this truth is not based upon one obscure passage of questionable meaning. In addition to the above passage from the book of Romans, we see this same principle clearly stated in at least four other passages (it is also at the heart of Matthew 25:31-46 which we will examine more closely in Chapter 4).

John 5:28-29 - *"Do not marvel at this; for an hour is coming, in which all who are in the tombs shall hear His voice, and shall come forth; those who did the* **good deeds** *to a resurrection of life, those who committed the* **evil deeds** *to a resurrection of judgment."* (NASB)

2 Corinthians 5:10 - *"For we must all appear before the judgment seat of Christ, that each one may be recompensed for his* **deeds** *in the body, according to what he has done, whether good or bad."* (NASB)

Revelation 20: 12 - *"And I saw the dead, the great and the small, standing before the throne, and books were opened; and another book was opened, which is the book of life; and the dead were judged from the things which were written in* *the books, according to their **deeds**."* (NASB)

Revelation 22:12 - *"Behold, I am coming quickly, and My wage is with Me to give to each according to his **deeds**."* (NASB)

This tension between being saved by grace through faith apart from any works and the clear teaching of being judged for our works is a tension which Scripture stubbornly refuses to resolve. As a result, when it comes to explaining this tension Evangelical Christians tend to make one of two mistakes.

Our first mistake is to minimize the importance of good deeds and the role they will play on the Day of Judgment. Indeed, our attitude is often down right dismissive. *"Don't be overly concerned,"* we tell inquisitive questioners, *"this doesn't affect your salvation. It's just about rewards for good behavior."* Let's be clear. Good deeds may not affect our salvation, but that does NOT mean they aren't important in the Kingdom of God, either now or on the Day of Judgment. Indeed, Scripture seems to clearly teach that where good deeds are absent in the life of a professing believer, salvation itself may be in question due to the absence of "fruit." It's time to realize that if good deeds are important enough for Scripture to warn us about their role on the Day of Judgment, they should be important enough for us to take them seriously.

Our second mistake is to limit good deeds to our favorite church or religious activities. Most Christians want to believe that when we appear before the Great Bema-Judgment seat

What Do The Scriptures Say?

of Christ He will judge us for such things as our outstanding Bible studies, our matchless men's conferences, our generous giving to the building fund drive, our faithful service teaching that Sunday School class or serving on that church committee. And I certainly don't want to minimize or disparage any of those worthwhile activities. Indeed, Paul says elsewhere that serving as a pastor/overseer in the Church is a "good deed" (see 1 Timothy 3:1).

But we need to ask ourselves if such church activities represent the sum total of what Scripture means by good deeds. After all, they aren't included in Matthew 25. And to my knowledge neither Jesus nor Paul ever served on a committee or church board. Or as a pastor friend of mine once wryly observed, *"The only board in Scripture is the one Paul floated to shore on!"* We need the spiritual courage to ask ourselves if our favorite church activities are functioning as a light to be seen by the world outside the confines of the Church and its four walls. Better to ask these tough questions now than to set yourself up for a rude awakening come Judgment Day!

Good Deeds Principle #6: Make Yourself Valuable!

For rulers are not a cause of fear for good behavior, but for evil. Do you want to have no fear of authority? Do what is good, and you will have praise from the same. (Romans 13:3)

About the time that William and Catherine Booth were laboring in the slums of London (in the mid-to-late 19th Century), Jozef de Veuster was stepping off a ship in

The Least Of These

Honolulu Harbor. Better known to history as Father Damian, he was a Catholic priest assigned to the Catholic Mission in North Kohala on the island of Hawai'i. When his Bishop announced a desire for a priest to minister to the needs of the 816 lepers living at the leper colony of Kalaupapa on Moloka'i, Father Damien gave it prayerful thought and then asked for permission to go to Moloka'I. In May of 1873 Bishop Maigret presented Damien to the leper colonists as *"one who will be a father to you, and who loves you so much that he does not hesitate to become one of you; to live and die with you."*

For the next eleven years Father Damian worked tirelessly to bring order out of chaos and basic medical treatment to the colony. Then, one evening in December of 1884, during

"The early Christians were known for both their morality and their compassion."

his evening ritual of soaking his feet in hot water, he realized that he could no longer feel the warmth of the water. He himself had become a leper. Father Damian continued to work among his "brother lepers" until his death in April, 1889. Canonized as a Saint in the Catholic Church in 1995 (the patron saint of lepers and those suffering from HIV/AIDS), Father Damian is a legend, both in his native Belgium as well as in Hawai'i. Through his ministry of good deeds among the lepers of Moloka'i, Father Damian made himself valuable to the community of Hawai'i, where his ministry is fondly remembered to this day. A statue of Father Damian stands outside the entrance to the Hawai'i State Capitol Building on the island of Oahu.

What Do The Scriptures Say?

The example of Father Damian is by no means an isolated example of Christians making themselves valuable to their communities (and becoming legendary in the process - see Chapter 10). Indeed, even during times of persecution under the Roman Empire the early Church was legendary for its good deeds, which came to the attention of both the average Roman and to the Roman rulers. The early Christians were known for both their morality and their compassion. When plague swept through the City of Rome and officials fled to the country, Christians remained behind and cared for the sick and dying. It was the Christians who searched the hills and bridges of Rome to find and rescue abandoned babies (a practice known as "exposure") and to raise them as their own. The pagan emperor Julian wrote, *"The impious Galileans support not only their poor, but ours as well, everyone can see that our people lack aid from us."* [25]

According to Dr. Gerald Sittser, *"As late as the middle of the fourth century the pagan emperor Julian complained that Christians had developed a massive social welfare system with which the pagan empire could not compete because the pagan worldview did not inspire people, as the Christian worldview did, to serve and sacrifice for the common good."*

I could cite many historical and contemporary examples of Christians walking in a Jesus-shaped spirituality, engaging in good deeds in the name of Christ and making themselves valuable to their communities. In a Presbyterian Church

---

[25]Gerald Sittser, *Water From A Deep Well: Christian Spirituality From Early Martyrs To Modern Missionaries*, (Downers Grove: IVP Books, 2007), page 56.

where my wife and I worshiped and served for several years I met a Christian family whose parents had been medical missionaries to mainland China during World War 2 and up until the Cultural Revolution and the expulsion of western missionaries. Their testimony and their work had made such an impact in the Province where they served that the Provincial Chinese government in the late 1990s invited all surviving members of the family to return to the Province to receive honors and recognition for the work their family had done on behalf of the Chinese people. They did this in the full knowledge that they were honoring the work of Christians in their midst! These Christians had made themselves valuable to that Chinese community through their good deeds in the name of Christ, so much so that even the pagan governing authorities could not help but acknowledge it.

As believers seeking to live out an authentic Jesus-shaped spirituality in our skeptical Postmodern culture, we need to once again make ourselves valuable to those around us through our good deeds.

Good Deeds Principle #7: Prepare To Be Stoned!

"The Jews picked up stones again to stone him. Jesus answered them, 'I have shown you many good works from the Father; for which of them are you going to stone me?'" (John 10:32-33)

O.K., it's time for a definition:

aphorism: 1. A tersely phrased statement of a truth or opinion; 2. A brief statement of a principle. Example: "No

What Do The Scriptures Say?

good deed will go unpunished."

If you and I are going to live out a Jesus-shaped spirituality of good deeds then we also need to be prepared for the "other" response which we see illustrated in this passage, and as expressed by one of my favorite aphorisms: *"No good deed will go unpunished"*!

The more I reflect on this passage, the more I understand a truth I had never really considered before. To illustrate this, let's begin by agreeing that Jesus, the incarnate Son of God did more and better works than anyone, either before or since. Are we agreed? And yet the religious leaders of His day wanted to stone Him, and eventually chose to put Him to death (John 11:49-50). Why was that? I believe there were two reasons.

The *first* reason, as John describes here, was theological. The religious leaders of Jesus' day, stumbled over Jesus' theological claims, specifically, His claim to be God incarnate. They stumbled over His theology, NOT His good works. This reminds me that chances are good that there will be people who will see our good deeds, maybe even appreciate them, but will stumble over our theology (you know, things like Jesus being the only way to God, conscious eternal punishment for unbelievers, etc.).

But Pastor and theologian R.C. Sproul offers us a *second* reason, one that goes deeper to the heart of the issue:

"The presence of Jesus represented the presence of the genuine in the midst of the bogus. Here authentic holiness

The Least Of These

*appeared; the counterfeiters of holiness were not pleased .
. . . Holiness provokes hatred. The greater the holiness, the
greater the human hostility toward it. It seems insane. No
man was ever more loving than Jesus Christ. Yet even His
love made people angry. His love was a perfect love, a
transcendent and holy love, but His very love brought trauma
to people. This kind of love is so majestic we can't stand it .
. . . So it was with Christ. The world could tolerate Jesus;
they could love Him, but only at a distance. Christ is safe for
us if securely bound by space and time. But a present Christ
could not survive in a world of hostile men. It was the
judgment of Caiaphas that, for the good of the nation, Jesus
must die."*[26]

There's an important point here that we as believers need to
grasp. When genuine believers pursuing a Jesus-shaped
spirituality express their obedience through good deeds it
tends to have an impact on people, including religious
people. A genuine Jesus-shaped spirituality confronts
religious people with a form of God's holiness which
threatens their self-made holiness and calls their religion-
shaped spirituality into question. To paraphrase Dr. Sproul's
observation, such a Jesus-shaped holiness is so majestic
that religious people can't stand it, except in small doses,
and then only at a distance. Their response is often to throw
"theological stones" (*"you've abandoned the true gospel of
the Kingdom for a mess of socialist pottage"*). That's O.K.
The same people wanted to stone Jesus. Why should they
treat you or me any better?!

---

[26]R.C. Sproul, **The Holiness of God**, pp. 64-71.

What Do The Scriptures Say?

Good Deeds Principle #8: Be Careful How You Walk

"And so, from the day we heard, we have not ceased to pray for you, asking that you may be filled with the knowledge of his will in all spiritual wisdom and understanding, so as to walk in a manner worthy of the Lord, fully pleasing to him, bearing fruit in every good work and increasing in the knowledge of God."(Colossians 1:9-10)

This passage is a grammatically complex sentence, and finding the point of a complex sentence can be a challenge. As any grammarian will tell you, it is always easier to understand a complex sentence if you diagram it into its clauses and components. I won't bore you with a diagram here. But based on my personal diagramming of this sentence, here is what I believe Paul is saying.

Paul prays for the believers in Colossae, asking that they be filled with a knowledge of God's will that will result in a personal walk with God which is both worthy of and pleasing to Him. Such a worthy walk, says Paul, will be characterized by two things: 1) bearing fruit in good deeds, and 2) an increasing knowledge of God.[27]

Much of the contemporary Evangelical Church is guilty of what I call *"a limping half-walk."* It is *"a limping half-walk"* because it is a walk strong on the *"increasing knowledge of*

---

[27]Grammatically, the verbs "bearing" and "increasing" are circumstantial participles modifying "walk," describing the circumstances in which the walk should occur.

The Least Of These

God" part, but it is woefully weak on the *"bearing fruit in every good work"* part. Now, don't get me wrong. It is a good thing for believers to be *"increasing in the knowledge of God."*

> *"Biblically speaking, knowledge without the fruit of obedience is 'useless.'"*

But biblically speaking, the purpose of knowledge is NOT to improve our education, but to inform and enlighten our obedience. When knowledge fails to increase and inform our obedience the result is "unfruitful knowledge." And Scripture warns against unfruitful knowledge, *"For if these qualities are yours and are increasing, they render you neither useless nor unfruitful in the true knowledge of our Lord Jesus Christ"* (2 Peter 1:8, NASB). Biblically speaking, knowledge without the fruit of obedience is "useless." [28]

So, how do we avoid "unfruitful knowledge"? By taking time to apply what we know through good deeds. I am convinced that the average Evangelical believer could take an immediate "sabbatical" from learning anything new about God or the Bible, and spend the rest of his or her life simply obeying what they already know. The crying need of the Church today is to move away from a religion-shaped spirituality which is built upon knowledge and programs, and to move into a Jesus-shaped spirituality which combines a genuine hunger for God with a personal walk of practical fruitfulness in good deeds. We need a spirituality which asks practical and personal questions such as, *"If I truly know*

---

[28] The English word "useless" is the Greek word *argos* meaning something which is "idle, barren or yielding no return due to inactivity.

What Do The Scriptures Say?

what Jesus would do in this situation, then why am I not doing it?"

Good Deeds Principle #9: Learn To Be Fruitful!

"And let our people also learn to engage in good deeds to meet pressing needs, that they may not be unfruitful." (Titus 3:14, NASB)

Biblical discipleship, the pursuit of a Jesus-shaped spirituality, is a life-long learning process. A disciple of the Kingdom is a life-long learner. And one of the things that he (or she) must learn is the

"In the teachings of Jesus the mark of genuine faith is not 'profession' but 'fruitfulness.'"

importance of good deeds and their role in being fruitful. The New Testament has much to say about bearing fruit. The concept of fruit or of bearing fruit occurs some 74 times in the New Testament, primarily in the gospels and the teachings of Jesus. In the teachings of Jesus the mark of genuine faith is not profession but fruitfulness. Based upon an alternative rendering of the Greek text, this passage could be translated as follows:

"And let our people learn about good deeds, namely, to take the lead in meeting pressing needs, in order that they may not be unfruitful."

This passage suggests three lessons which every Jesus-shaped disciple of the Kingdom needs to learn.

The Least Of These

First, we need to learn to *"take the lead"* in doing good deeds. The sense of the Greek verb translated "engage in"[29] is *"to make something one's business,"* hence, to *"take the lead."* When it comes to good deeds we need to *"make it our business"* to be pro-active, not passive. We should be leading, not following.

Second, we need to learn to meet *"pressing needs"* (literally, "indispensable necessities"). Some commentators argue that Paul is simply urging Titus to tell his people to work hard to meet the daily needs of their own family. While this passage could be construed that way, our alternative translation suggests that this is not an exclusive or necessary interpretation.

Such a narrow interpretation raises questions. For example, how is a professing believer working hard to provide for himself and his family more of a testimony than a non-believer working hard to provide for his own family? And why would Christians need to "learn" to do this? Providing for one's own family comes natural. Even unbelievers do that (see our earlier comments on Luke 6:32-36 in Chapter 2). But engaging in good deeds to meet the pressing needs of others is something that must be taught and learned.

I believe Paul is telling Titus that believers pursuing a Jesus-

---

[29]Greek: *proistemi* - In the Greek of the 1st century this word had a varied usage, including to preside, to rule or govern, to engage in aggressively, to take the lead and to make it one's business. See J.H. Moulton and G. Milligan, ***The Vocabulary of the Greek Testament Illustrated from the Papyri and Other Non-Literary Sources*** (London: Hodder & Stoughton, 1914-1930), page 541.

What Do The Scriptures Say?

shaped spirituality need to be taught the importance of identifying and meeting the pressing needs of those around them as a testimony of Christ-like good deeds.

This, of course, raises the practical question of whether you and I even know the pressing needs of those around us who may be in a position of being unable to provide for themselves. How many people with "pressing needs" do you know and could reach out to in the name of Christ?

> *"In the economy of Jesus, the mark of a good tree is the good fruit it produces. And the mark of a bad tree is the absence of fruit. Which are you? And which am I?"*

Third, we need to take seriously the emphasis upon not being unfruitful. We encountered this idea earlier with respect to "unfruitful knowledge." Scripture makes a big deal about between being *"fruitful in every good work"* (Colossians 1:10) as opposed to being *"unfruitful"* (i.e., the absence of good works). Fruitfulness is good. Unfruitfulness is bad. Healthy trees are fruitful. Unhealthy trees are unfruitful. Unfruitful vines are pruned and their

> *". . . our deeds, whether good or bad, are the most obvious testimony as to our true spiritual condition."*

branches are tossed into the fire (John 15:1-6). Unfruitful trees are uprooted and burned (Matthew 7:17-19). In the economy of Jesus, the mark of a good tree is the good fruit it produces. And the mark of a bad tree is the absence of

The Least Of These

fruit. Which are you? And which am I?

Good Deeds Principle #10: You Can't Hide!

"The sins of some people are conspicuous, going before them to judgment, but the sins of others appear later. So also good works are conspicuous, and even those that are not cannot remain hidden." (1 Timothy 5:24-25)

Let's be real for just a moment. Most professing Christians live in denial of a fundamental spiritual reality: our deeds, whether good or bad, are the most obvious testimony as to our true spiritual condition. Think about it this way. Our theology tells people what

> *"Our theology tells people what we think about God in theory. Our deeds tell people what we believe about God (and about other people) in reality."*

we think about God in theory. Our deeds tell people what we believe about God (and about other people) in reality. Our authentic deeds reveal our authentic selves in a way that everyone can see, warts and all. In other words, we are what we do.

The nature of everyone's "spirituality" tends to be self revealing through the fruit it produces. The fruit of a genuine Jesus-shaped spirituality is good deeds which look like Jesus and sound like the Kingdom of God. They shine a light in the darkness and cause men to glorify God. The fruit of a religion-shaped spirituality is deeds which highlight religious activities and programs, and which serve the purpose of

What Do The Scriptures Say?

causing men to think well of our "church."

> "Your deeds are your fruit - your light - and the strongest testimony to those around you that you are, indeed, a 'disciple of the Kingdom.'"

Paul's warning to Timothy is simple: Your deeds will eventually "out" you. The good deeds of a Jesus-shaped spirituality will become "evident."[30] And the "unfruitful" deeds of a religion-shaped spirituality are *"unable to be hidden."* In simple terms, we can't hide behind our deeds, because our deeds will eventually reveal us for who we really are.

These are sobering realities which should force each of us to examine the kind of deeds we are doing, why we are doing them, what kind of fruit we are producing and how it is being viewed by those around us. Who is being glorified? Me? My ministry? My church? Or Jesus? Your deeds are your fruit - your light - and the strongest testimony to those around you that you are, indeed, a *"disciple of the Kingdom."*

Good Deeds Principle #11: Do Our Deeds Match Our Words?

*"To the pure, all things are pure, but to the defiled and unbelieving, nothing is pure; but both their minds and their consciences are defiled. They **profess** to know God, but they **deny** him by their works. They are detestable, disobedient, unfit for any good work."* (Titus 1:15-16)

---

[30]Greek: *prodelos* - plain, obvious, openly evident

The Least Of These

The New Testament book of Titus is one of three "pastoral epistles" (1 and 2 Timothy being the other two), letters which the Apostle Paul wrote to

> *"Do the deeds of our life match up with the words of our profession."*

young organic house church leaders to help them with some of the practical issues of personal discipleship and church life which were arising in their ministries. It is worth noting that it is in one of these pastoral letters that Paul gives his most extensive treatment of the importance of good deeds. [31]

The irritating thing about practical questions is that they tend to expose practical problems. For example, consider this question: *"Do the deeds of our life match up with the words of our profession."* That's the practical question Paul seems to be addressing in this passage. You've heard it said before. In fact, you have probably said it yourself at one time or another. *"He (or she) talks the talk, but they don't walk the walk."* Biblically speaking, as we will soon learn from Paul's words to Titus, this is a major problem. The problem is one of on-going personal inconsistency involving a person who professes to be a believer in Jesus, but whose life and deeds give little or no outward evidence of inward transformation.

This problem of "talk" versus "walk" may be rampant in the Church today, but it certainly is not new. Paul and the early Church were well aware of it. And here Paul warns his disciple and protégée, Titus, against people who *"profess to*

---

[31]The book of Titus contains five separate references to the issue of good deeds in the life of the believer and the Church: Titus 1:16; 2:7; 2:14; 3:1 and 3:14.

What Do The Scriptures Say?

know God" on the one hand, but who *"by their deeds . . . deny Him."* Paul describes such people as being *"worthless for any good deed."* The Greek word rendered "worthless" (_adokimos_) is used outside the New Testament to describe metals or coins which have failed to pass the test of genuineness - they are "counterfeit." Professing believers whose deeds do not match their profession are like debased coins or counterfeit currency - worthless. They are NOT what they claim to be. In simple terms, Paul is warning Titus against people whose profession of faith is nothing more than fool's gold masquerading as the real thing.

Paul offers up a harsh dose of spiritual reality, born out of many years of personal experience. There are people in the midst of our fellowships who are counterfeit Christians. Debased coins. Fool's gold. They use all the right words

> *"Professing believers whose deeds do not match their profession are like debased coins or counterfeit currency - worthless."*

and are fluent in "Christian speak," but their deeds deny Him, contradict their words, and show their faith to be fool's gold. At the end of the day, we must decide which to believe, their words or their deeds (fruit). Scripture leans toward deeds over words. Why? Because over time, what we do is a function of who we are. Good trees produce good fruit. Good people produce good deeds. That's how it works. Beware fool's gold masquerading as faith.

The Least Of These

Good Deeds Principle #12: Be A Model

"Likewise, urge the younger men to be self-controlled. Show yourself in all respects to be a model of good works, and in your teaching show integrity, dignity, and sound speech that cannot be condemned, so that an opponent may be put to shame, having nothing evil to say about us." (Titus 2:6-8)

It is difficult to exhort and encourage others to take spiritual things seriously if the circumstances of our own lives are out of control. This is Paul's leadership challenge to Titus. Paul reminds Titus that leaders in the Church must lead by example, not just by exhortation. This comes out more clearly in the Greek text which could be rendered as follows:

"Likewise, Titus, encourage the young men to be serious minded in all things, while at the same time you show yourself to be a model of good deeds."

As leaders, if we want others to engage in good deeds, then we must give them a model to follow. The Greek word translated "example" (*tupos*) is a bit more technical. It originally referred to the mark left by a blow or the impress of a

> *"The challenge of biblical leadership is to be a model - a spiritual 'die-stamp' - which leaves an indelible impression on the lives of others."*

seal or the stamp of a coin. It came to refer to the die-stamp from which other copies were made. This gave way to the idea of an original pattern, mould or model, which is how Paul uses the word here. The challenge of biblical leadership is to be a model - a spiritual "die-stamp" - which leaves an

What Do The Scriptures Say?

indelible impression on the lives of others. And the impression Paul exhorts Titus to leave on those around him is the importance of engaging in good deeds.

As believers seeking to authentically live out a Jesus-shaped spirituality, Jesus Himself is our model and "die-stamp." It is His model of accomplishing those works which the Father gave Him to do that we seek to emulate. It is the "die-stamp" of His compassion and good deeds which makes an indelible impression upon us and challenges us to do the same in the lives of those around us. When it comes to good deeds, what kind of "die-stamp" are you on the lives of those around you?

Good Deeds Principle #13: Be Zealous!

"For the grace of God has appeared, bringing salvation for all people, training us to renounce ungodliness and worldly passions, and to live self-controlled, upright, and godly lives in the present age, waiting for our blessed hope, the appearing of the glory of our great God and Savior Jesus Christ, who gave himself for us to redeem us from all lawlessness and to purify for himself a people for his own possession who are zealous for good works." (Titus 2:11-14)

This passage immediately presents us with a question: What exactly does it mean to be "zealous"?[32] The answer to that question requires some explaining. In first century Judaism there existed a group of people know as "the Zealots." These

---

[32]The term "Zealot" (in Hebrew *kanai* - frequently used in plural form, *kana'im*), means *"one who is zealous on behalf of God."* The Greek equivalent is *zelotes*, which describes an emulator, a zealous admirer or follower."

The Least Of These

were radical Jews who worked hard to incite the people of Judah to rebel against the Roman Empire and expel it from Palestine by force. The Jewish historian Josephus described the Zealots as one of the "four sects" at that time, the other three being the Pharisees, the Sadducees, and the Essenes. According to Josephus, the Zealots *"agree in all other things with the Pharisaic notions; but they have an inviolable attachment to liberty, and say that God is to be their only Ruler and Lord."* [33] The Zealots opposed Roman rule by targeting Romans and Greeks for assassination. Other Zealots, known as the Sicarii, engaged in violence against other Jews, killing those they considered apostate and collaborators, while urging Jews to fight Roman occupation. The Zealots were instrumental in the Jewish Revolt of A.D. 66, seizing Jerusalem and holding it until A.D. 70, when the Roman General Titus, son of Emperor Vespasian, retook the city, sold the survivors into slavery and destroyed Herod's Temple. Jesus had a disciple who was a former Zealot.[34]

The Jewish Zealots of the first century embodied a radical commitment to and jealousy for God and Jewish nationalism. It was misplaced, but it was genuine. This is the background that would have colored any first-century reader of Paul's letter to Titus. Paul's readers would have recognized and understood the problem of mis-placed zeal. But Paul now urges Christians to demonstrate this kind of radical commitment and jealousy when it comes to good deeds. He wants them to become "zealots," not for mis-placed

---

[33]Flavius Josephus, **Antiquities**, 18.1.6)

[34]Simon the Zealot. His name appears in all four "official" lists of Jesus' disciples: Matthew 10:4; Mark 3:18; Luke 6:15 & Acts 1:13

What Do The Scriptures Say?

nationalism but for good deeds in the name of Jesus.

This passage draws a contrast between "lawless deeds," such as those of the political Zealots of that day, and the "good deeds" Christians should be engaging in. Believers in pursuit of a Jesus-shaped spirituality should be "zealous," but for good deeds. So, I have to ask myself: Am I a zealot for good deeds? Am I as zealous for a Jesus-shaped spirituality of good deeds as the Zealots of the first century were in their mis-guided pursuit of politics and religion? Does my life demonstrate a radical commitment to and jealousy for those good deeds which God has prepared for me to walk in?

According to Paul in this passage, this is what Jesus died for! Paul argues that our redemption is two-fold: We have been redeemed **FROM** sin, and we have been redeemed **FOR** good deeds. I often wonder if the reason we are not more

"Redemption in Scripture is always purposeful. We are not simply saved FROM something. We are also saved FOR something."

zealous FOR good deeds is because most of us don't really appreciate what we have been saved FROM. Redemption in Scripture is always purposeful. We are not simply saved FROM something (i.e., from conscious eternal punishment for our sin in hell). We are also saved FOR something. We have been redeemed for good deeds, deeds which call for radical commitment and "zeal" on our part as we pursue a Jesus-shaped spirituality.

The Least Of These

Good Deeds Principle #14: Set The Tone!

"This is a trustworthy statement; and concerning these things I want you to speak confidently, so that those who have believed God may be careful to engage in good deeds. These things are good and profitable for men" (Titus 3:8, NASB).

It is a spiritual reality that the gifted leadership of the Church (see particularly Ephesians 4:7-13) is tasked by God with setting the spiritual tone for others to follow. Allow me a clumsy but practical example. I've been privileged to attend a few symphony performances, and have watched a few more on TV. There is a "ritual" they go through which has always fascinated me and which I think is instructive. When the orchestra members first enter the stage they will sit for a while testing their instruments and shuffling their music sheets. But there is an empty seat, reserved for the "first chair" or "first violin." When this person walks onto the stage and takes their seat, the orchestra starts to quiet down. Then, at a certain moment, the "first chair" will take their instrument and play a single note. As that note resonates across the stage each instrumental section begins to pick up that note and play it until the entire orchestra is resonating that one note. Why? Because the entire orchestra is tuning itself to that note. When the ritual is complete the entire orchestra is in tune with one another and the performance can begin. It is at this point that the conductor enters the stage, takes his position and begins to conduct the entire orchestra.

Without getting carried away let's apply this example to the

What Do The Scriptures Say?

Church. Jesus is the Conductor. The Church of assembled believers is the orchestra. God's gifted leaders are "the first chair." And the unbelieving, watching world is the audience waiting to hear our performance! I don't know about you, but I'm genuinely wondering what's going to happen next! But, notice. In this example it isn't the function of "the first chair" to carry the entire performance. And who wants to go to a symphonic concert just to hear the first violin guy (or girl) tune his instrument?! I want to hear the entire symphony play all of their instruments, don't you?!

In this passage from Titus, the Apostle Paul points out that leaders like Titus have been tasked with a responsibility regarding good deeds. As a "first chair" in this divine symphony Titus has a responsibility to set the tone for those he serves, who are listening and waiting to tune their instruments to his note. Paul reminds Titus that, as a leader seeking to model a Jesus-shaped spirituality to those around him, Titus needs to "insist" concerning the importance of good deeds in the life of the believer and the Church. The sense of the Greek verb translated "insist" (*diabebaioomai*) is to firmly assert something to the point of insisting on it.

> "Jesus is the Conductor. The Church of assembled believers is the orchestra. God's gifted leaders are 'the first chair.' And the unbelieving, watching world is the audience waiting to hear our performance!"

Few things confuse people more than indecision or a lack of clarity among leadership. A confused tone will produce a confused orchestra. As Paul told the Corinthian believers, *"if the bugle produces an indistinct sound, who will prepare himself for battle?"* (1 Corinthians 14:8).The Greek word translated "be careful" literally means *"to exercise careful thought."*[35] When combined here with the word "engage" [36] the idea is that, as a result of Titus' clear insistent teaching, those around him will be challenged to think carefully about how to make good deeds their business and to practice them. So, here is my "alternate translation" of this passage,

"Concerning these things, I want you to be insistent, so that those who have believed God might exercise careful thought concerning how to make good deeds their business."

This type of clear insistence would lead to such practical questions as: Who needs help? What can we do? How can we do more? How can we challenge others to do more? What would Jesus do if He were here facing this situation?

"Few things confuse people more than indecision or a lack of clarity among leadership. A confused tone will produce a confused orchestra."

Good Deeds Principle #15: Stimulate One Another

"Let us hold fast the confession of our hope without wavering, for he who promised is faithful. And let us consider

---

[35]*phrontizo* - used only here in the New Testament

[36]*proistemi* - literally, "to make it one's business" - which we saw earlier when we looked at "Good Deeds Principle #9

What Do The Scriptures Say?

how to stir up one another to love and good works, not neglecting to meet together, as is the habit of some, but encouraging one another, and all the more as you see the Day drawing near." (Hebrews 10:23-25)

Let's ask ourselves a simple, basic question: Why do you go to Church? Why do you gather together with other believers? Do you go to Church for the great Bible teaching? For the awesome worship music? For the exciting children's ministry? For the dynamic youth ministry? For fellowship with other believers? These can all be good things. But, according to the writer of Hebrews, one of the primary reasons why believers should gather together is to "consider" how we can "stir up" each other to good deeds. The Greek verb translated "consider" (*katanoeo*) carries the sense of understanding something after careful study. And the English rendering of "stir up" doesn't quite do justice to the Greek word *paroxumos* which communicates the idea of "inciting" or "provoking" someone to the point of sharp disagreement. One of the purposes of assembling together as believers is so that we can give careful thought and study as to how we can incite and provoke one another to good deeds.

The verbiage of this passage should lead us to ask and answer a question: Just how much thought do you put into how to best incite those around you to good deeds? If we aren't provoking and inciting one another to greater love and good deeds, then we aren't fulfilling one of the primary Scriptural reasons for gathering as the Church.

A mega church in our city with an attendance of over 6,000 people decided they needed to do something to challenge their people to good deeds. So, the leadership made a

The Least Of These

decision to purchase 5,000 copies of Richard Stern's excellent book, *The Hole In Our Gospel* and to distribute them free to the congregation. Richard Stern is President of WorldVision USA and the book is the story of his personal journey into good deeds. The pastor spent several weeks preaching through the book while the book was read and studied in small groups. On the final Sunday of the series the Church invited the author to speak. I was present, and Stern's message was quite good. The congregation in each of the three morning services was challenged to personally sponsor over 1,500 impoverished children in third world countries. Fifteen hundred sponsorship slips were taped to the auditorium wall and people were encouraged to pray about it, take one and sponsor a child. Well before the last morning service, all 1,500 slips were gone. It was a thoughtful, powerful and effective way of stimulating one another to greater love and good deeds.

Well done!

As we gather together as organic churches, we need to ask ourselves what we can do to prod one another to greater obedience and good deeds.

Reflections For A Jesus-Shaped Spirituality

O.K., are you bored yet, or are you simply overwhelmed?! More importantly, have you gotten the point about the importance of good deeds in the life of the believer in pursuit of a Jesus-shaped spirituality? There are more Scriptures we could look at to make our point, but sometimes "more is less." In the interest of time (and keeping what's left of your

What Do The Scriptures Say?

attention) I'll simply summarize them: Scripture urges us to *"be rich in good deeds"* (Timothy 6:17-19); to *"be prepared for good deeds"* (2 Timothy 2:21); to *"be equipped for good deeds"* (2 Timothy 3:16-17); to *"be ready for good deeds"* (Titus 3:1-2); and finally Scripture reminds us that good deeds and good words must go together (2 Thessalonians 2:16-17).

By now the Biblical point should be clear. Good deeds are important in the life of both the individual believer and the Church. They represent the indispensable fruit of the believing life and experience; the outward manifestation of a Jesus-shaped spirituality. But much of the Church has forgotten both to teach and to practice this biblical truth. As we have seen, biblical leaders should be insisting on this to the point of provoking the Church to irritation. It really is that important. But because of our neglect, our Postmodern culture has gone its own way, having concluded that it can manifest good deeds without Jesus. For its part, the Church has concluded that it can manifest Jesus without good deeds. Our Postmodern culture's plan seems to be working. The Church's plan is a disaster. What's your plan?

The Least Of These

Reflection Question # 1 - What are some of the lessons you have learned from this Chapter about good deeds in the New Testament?

Reflection Question # 2 - What "Good Deeds Principle" stood out to you as something you had not considered before?

Reflection Question # 3 - List some things you plan to do or behaviors you plan to change as a result of what you have learned from this Chapter.

What Do The Scriptures Say?

15 Biblical Principles Concerning Good Deeds	
Passage	*Principle*
John 5: 38	Our Works Are Our Witness
Matthew 5:14-26	Be A Light
Ephesians 2:8-10	Find Your Purpose
2 Corinthians 9:7-9	Learn To Overflow
Romans 2:5-10	Judgment Day Is Coming
Romans 13:3	Make Yourself Valuable
John 10:32-33	Prepare To Be Stoned
Colossians 1:9-10	Be Careful How You Walk
Titus 3:14	Learn To Be Fruitful
1 Timothy 5:24-25	You Can't Hide
Titus 1: 15-16	Do Our Deeds Match Our Words
Titus 2:6-8	Be A Model
Titus 2:11-14	Be Zealous
Titus 3:8	Set The Tone
Hebrews 10:23-25	Stimulate One Another

The Least Of These

Chapter 5

Reflections On "The Least of These"

"When the Son of Man comes in his glory, and all the angels with him, then he will sit on his glorious throne. Before him will be gathered all the nations, and he will separate people one from another as a shepherd separates the sheep from the goats. And he will place the sheep on his right, but the goats on the left. Then the King will say to those on his right, 'Come, you who are blessed by my Father, inherit the kingdom prepared for you from the foundation of the world. For I was hungry and you gave me food, I was thirsty and you gave me drink, I was a stranger and you welcomed me, I was naked and you clothed me, I was sick and you visited me, I was in prison and you came to me.' Then the righteous will answer him, saying, Lord, when did we see you hungry and feed you, or thirsty and give you drink? And when did we see you a stranger and welcome you, or naked and clothe you? And when did we see you sick or in prison and visit you?' And the King will answer them, 'Truly, I say to you, as you did it to one of the least of these my brothers, you did it to me.' Then he will say to those on his left, 'Depart from me, you cursed, into the eternal fire prepared for the devil and his angels. For I was hungry and you gave me no food, I was thirsty and you gave me no drink, I was a stranger and you did not welcome me, naked and you did not clothe me, sick and in prison and you did not visit me.' Then they also will answer, saying, 'Lord, when did we see you hungry or thirsty or a stranger or naked or sick or in prison, and did not

The Least Of These

minister to you?' Then he will answer them, saying, 'Truly, I say to you, as you did not do it to one of the least of these, you did not do it to me.' And these will go away into eternal punishment, but the righteous into eternal life." (Matthew 25:31-46)

A Funny Thing Happened
On My Way To The Conference . . .

It happened while I was on my way to an organic church conference in Ontario, California, sponsored by Church Multiplication Associates. It was a good conference. And, as always, it was good to see old house church friends, get caught up on life's comings and going, and to get challenged by some excellent speakers. I was one week into a 40-day fast (for Lent), which made it somewhat awkward around meal times, but after 12 years of doing this I had come to accept it as one of the socially awkward consequences of obedience.

But my biggest experience of the weekend took place on the airplane on my way to the conference. People who read my almost-weekly e-letters (which you can subscribe to on our website at risingrivermedia.org) already know that these things tend to happen to me on the way to conferences. Caution. Don't volunteer to travel with me unless you want God to teach you a lesson along the way (Hmmm. Something going on there)! As I flew out of Spokane I decided to spend the one hour trip to Portland by having devotions. I chose to read a familiar passage that God had recently impressed on me: Matthew 25:31-46. But this time I decided to spot-translate the passage out of the Greek. So

Reflections On "The Least of These"

I pulled my Reader's Greek New Testament (a gift from my daughter) out of my backpack and began to read. And that's when it happened. Before I finished the passage I found myself weeping. And, I suppose, that needs an explanation.

Now, mind you, Greek can bring a person to tears for several reasons. It tends to happen frequently among first year Greek students when confronted by a Greek teacher who calls them to the front of the class, hands them a quarter and says, *"Call home and tell your parents you'll never be a Greek scholar."* Yep, that'll do it.

But this was different. As I read the Greek text and began to appreciate the nuances of what I found there, I began to sense the Holy Spirit convicting me of how poorly I had understood this passage before now. Left to our own devices we all tend to interpret Scripture in that way which best suits or agrees with our preconceived understanding of the world. Yes, sometimes we only see what we want to see. We need fresh illumination by the Holy Spirit to open our eyes, give us new perspective and enable us to see what was always there. I don't want to belabor this point, or bore you with a Bible study which is only meaningful to me, but I want to briefly share just a few of these new-to-me insights.

Fresh Insights on Matthew 25

Insight # 1:   This Passage Isn't So Much a "Parable" as a Description. Parables were illustrated stories drawn from everyday life, which both revealed and concealed spiritual truth. Some of them were downright hard to understand without added explanation. Just ask the Disciples who were

The Least Of These

constantly asking Jesus, *"What did you mean?"* That isn't the case here. This passage is a description of what is going to happen on the Day of Judgment as Jesus ("the Son of Man") comes in glory and sits on His glorious throne. To spend

> *"It's Judgment Day. Jesus is on His throne. And we're all about to be judged. The question we should be asking ourselves at this point is, 'Judged for what?'"*

endless word studies on the meaning and significance of a "throne" is to miss the point. It's Judgment Day. Jesus is on His throne. And we're all about to be judged. The question we should be asking ourselves at this point is, *"Judged for what?"* Now, that is simple and straightforward . . . even in the Greek.

Insight # 2: We Are Trapped by Our "Religious Vocabulary." I saw this in Verse 34 in the phrase "blessed of My Father." In the various ways we tend to use it, the word "blessed" usually conjures up warm religious feelings and notions among professing believers. As Christians we tend to throw around the word "blessing" without ever thinking beyond how religious and spiritual it makes us feel. In other words, we are trapped in our religious vocabulary, unable to see past our "religious feelings" to the actual meaning of what's being said.

The Greek word for blessing here (*eulogeo*) simply means *"to speak well of"* someone or something. Do you really want to "bless" me? Then stop talking about me behind my back and begin to "speak well" of me instead (Sorry, just had to throw that in there!). The phrase *"blessed of my Father"* in this passage should cause us to ask ourselves a question: Do we want to be *'spoken well of'* by God on the Day of Judgment?

> *"Do we want to be 'spoken well of' by God on the Day of Judgment?"*

If we do, then we might want to pay attention to the rest of this passage, because it sets forth the terms and conditions for that to happen.

O.K., at this point you might be asking yourself, *"What's the alternative to being spoken well of by God."* We find that in verse 41: *"Then he will say to those on his left, 'Depart from me, you cursed, into the eternal fire prepared for the devil and his angels.'"* There it is. The alternative to being spoken well of by God is to be told to "depart from me" and to be called "cursed" by that same God. Now, if you can find a positive way to spin being told by God to "go away from Me" and being called "cursed" (not to mention the whole eternal fire part) knock yourself out. I can't.

There you have it. A clear separation between those who will be "well spoken of" (i.e., "blessed") by God, and those who will be called "cursed" by that same God. The remainder of this passage explains how and why this separation takes place.

Insight # 3: God's Concern Should Be Our Concern. I was struck by the phrase "you visited me" in verse 36. The Greek word "visited" carries the idea of examining something very closely.[37] When applied to relationships it carries the force of *"to show such concern for someone's welfare that you go looking for them and check on their condition."* And there's the rub. When was the last time you were so

> *". . . it's difficult to engage in good deeds toward those in need if we haven't made the effort to search them out and discover exactly what it is that they need."*

concerned for someone who was hungry, naked (poorly clothed), a stranger (lonely), sick, imprisoned or otherwise marginalized that you went out of your way to seek them out, to find them and to check on their welfare. In the context of our discussion concerning good deeds, it's difficult to engage in good deeds toward those in need if we haven't made the effort to search them out and discover exactly what it is that they need. Laziness and zealousness simply do not travel well together.

Perhaps you remember the story from the fourth chapter of Genesis. In a fit of jealous rage, Cain killed his brother Abel. When God visited Cain and inquired as to where Abel might be, Cain responded with what has become a classic and timeless question, *"Am I my brother's keeper?"* The answer to Cain's question would wait more than 2,000 years until Jesus Himself answered it in Matthew 25. And the answer is, "Yes!" We are our brother's keeper. And that's the point of this passage. God's concern should be our concern. He is

---

[37]Greek: *episkeptomai* - from the root *skeptomai*, referring to a watch or a sentry, and from which we get our word "skeptic." The prefix *epi* serves to intensify the meaning of the root.

concerned with the well-being of those around us: the hungry, the naked, the poor, the prisoner, the stranger, the sick, the marginalized. The real question is this: Do we share that concern?

> *"We are our brother's keeper. And that's the point of this passage. God's concern should be our concern."*

Insight # 4: Fattening People Up Is a Good Thing. Over my years of reading Greek (started in college) I've come to appreciate some of the nuances of the language. For example, in verse 37 we read *"Lord, when did we see you hungry (i.e., in a continual state of being hungry) and feed you."* The Greek word "feed" (*trepho*) means *"to fatten, to pamper, to rear, to bring up, to nourish."* This isn't simply feeding hungry people. This is pampering them with food to the point of fattening them up! As I was writing this I couldn't help but think of the sitcom *"Everybody Loves Raymond"* where Ray's Italian mother (Marie) was constantly forcing food on him, *"You're looking pale, son. Let me fix you something to eat."* For Marie, food wasn't simply food. It was a way of expressing genuine love and concern.

During the same period of time when I traveled to the Organic Church Conference mentioned earlier, I was also responsible for feeding 30-to-40 men at a local homeless men's shelter every Thursday night. One of my first tasks when I arrived home from the Conference was to go on my weekly "food hunt." I called one of my local food sources. When she informed me that she had a dozen beef roasts I nearly dropped the phone. *"I'll meet you in 20 minutes and*

The Least Of These

pick them up," I blurted out. Cooked overnight in BBQ sauce those roasts would fall apart into pulled beef BBQ sandwiches. Add a couple pans of small red potatoes and mixed vegetables and the guys would be eating well Thursday night. When I cook, I want them to eat as well at the shelter as I do at home . . . sometimes even better. Why? Because I think that's what Jesus meant when he said, *"When I was hungry you fed me."* As in all good deeds done in the name of Jesus as an expression of our Jesus-shaped spirituality, we need to learn to abound, to overflow. Not to simply "get by."

Insight # 5: When Did That Become My Ministry? The insights I've shared so far were powerful and I was deeply struck by them. But they really didn't prepare me for what came next. I found "it" at the end of verse 44. The English reads, *"When did we see you . . . . and not take care of you."* In the Greek, the phrase *"take care of you"* is the word <u>diakoneo</u>. Yes, we get our English word "deacon" from this one. This word means *"to wait on or serve someone, to act as a deacon, to minister."*

Again, because we often get trapped in our religious vocabulary - words like deacon or serve - we miss the force of what is really being said. What these people (i.e., the goats) were asking Jesus was simply this, *"When did feeding the hungry, clothing the naked, visiting the prisoner,*

> *"These things became your ministry the day you decided that you wanted to be well spoken of by God on the Day of Judgment."*

Reflections On Matthew 25

seeing to the sick; when did these things become my ministry, Lord?" Haven't you ever asked that same question? Be honest. Of course you have. And here is the answer: These things became your ministry the day you decided that you wanted to be well spoken of by God on the Day of Judgment. These things became your ministry the day you decided to pursue a Jesus-shaped spirituality.

Insight # 6: This Stuff Is Important Enough to Have Eternal Consequences. For a growing number of professing believers today, Christianity is increasingly becoming a spiritual form of no-fault car insurance. No one gets blamed for anything and everything gets fixed in the end. Just pay your premium (tithing?) and life will be good.

But when we read this passage in Matthew we are confronted with a very different and stark reality. We are responsible and accountable for our actions or in-actions, all of which h a v e   e t e r n a l consequences. It is a fact of

> *"Compassion, missions and the Christian life are all inextricably tied to the reality of accountability and consequences, both immediate and eternal."*

Church history that whenever the Church has lost its sense of accountability and the eternal consequences of its actions or non-actions, the results have always been disastrous. If good deeds have no eternal consequences, why bother with them? After all, they are often inconvenient and involve hard, messy work. The same is true of missions. Don't worry about the lost, because they'll all get saved eventually by a loving God (the view of Universalism). Compassion, missions and the Christian life are all inextricably tied to the reality of accountability and consequences, both immediate and eternal. Get over it. Once we grasp the reality of judgment and accountability as presented in this passage, we must next grasp the reality that our practice of good deeds (such as feeding the hungry, clothing the naked, welcoming the stranger, visiting the prisoner, attending the sick, reaching out to the marginalized) has eternal consequences. Personally, I want to be spoken well of by God on the Day of Judgment, and if that requires the fear of eternal consequences in order to overcome my natural slothfulness and to jolt me out of my sense of "no fault insurance Christianity," well, so be it.

Reflections For A Jesus-Shaped Spirituality

Don't be surprised when your pursuit of a Jesus-shaped spirituality leads you to the hungry, the naked, the stranger, the prisoner, the sick and the marginalized. That's where it led Jesus. And that's where He expects it to lead us.

Reflection Question # 1 - What did you learn from this passage in Matthew 25 that you did not know before?

Reflection Question # 2 - Discuss how *"God's concern should be our concern."*

Reflections On Matthew 25

Reflection Question # 3 - What have you learned from this Chapter that would lead you to conclude that you and I really are our brother's keeper? How does this reality impact our responsibility to engage in good deeds.

Reflection Question # 4 - Based on what you have learned from this Chapter, when did ministry to *"the least of these"* become your responsibility?

Reflection Question # 5 - If you genuinely believe that your good deeds will somehow have eternal consequences, how will that belief change your behavior today, and what do you plan to do differently?

The Least Of These

Chapter 6

The Unforgivable Sin of Divorce

"Is not this the fast that I choose: to loose the bonds of wickedness, to undo the straps of the yoke, to let the oppressed go free, and to break every yoke? Is it not to share your bread with the hungry and bring the homeless poor into your house; when you see the naked, to cover him, and not to hide yourself from your own flesh? Then shall your light break forth like the dawn, and your healing shall spring up speedily; your righteousness shall go before you; the glory of the LORD shall be your rear guard. Then you shall call, and the LORD will answer; you shall cry, and he will say, 'Here I am.' If you take away the yoke from your midst, the pointing of the finger, and speaking wickedness, if you pour yourself out for the hungry and satisfy the desire of the afflicted, then shall your light rise in the darkness and your gloom be as the noonday. And the LORD will guide you continually and satisfy your desire in scorched places and make your bones strong; and you shall be like a watered garden, like a spring of water, whose waters do not fail. And your ancient ruins shall be rebuilt; you shall raise up the foundations of many generations; you shall be called the repairer of the breach, the restorer of streets to dwell in." (Isaiah 58:6-12).

"Empty Stomach, Full Heart"

It all began innocently enough with an e-mail and a phone call. At the time I was serving as the Executive Director of

The Least Of These

Feed Spokane, a food rescue agency which I had co-founded. The Lent season was approaching and I had decided to do something out-of-the-ordinary, at least for me. I had decided to do a *public* 40-day fast on behalf of the hungry and the homeless in our city. Over the preceding 12 years or so (since 1995) I had engaged in two 40-day fasts every year as part of my personal spiritual disciplines (long story). But this one was different. Those had been private. This fast would be very public in order to draw attention to the plight of on-going hunger and homelessness in our city. I announced it in a simple e-mail to my 150 or so Feed Spokane meal site coalition contacts. A friend at the local newspaper saw the e-mail, called me and we did a quick interview over the phone. The result appeared as a front page article in the local newspaper entitled *"Empty Stomach, Full Heart."* [38]

Scripture offers many examples and reasons for fasting. I've personally identified more than forty examples, and nearly as many reasons. I had fasted regularly for more than twelve years and had written two books on the topic before the truth of Isaiah 58 fully dawned on me. Yep, I can be a little slow, but I do eventually catch on.

Over the years I had come to understand fasting as an act of profound personal repentance before a holy God who opposes the proud, but gives grace to the humble. I had also come to know fasting as a profound act of personal sacrificial worship before a God Who seeks those who will worship Him

---

[38]As of this writing, the article was still available on-line at http://www.spokesman.com/stories/2008/feb/05/empty-stomach-full-heart-on-fasting/

The Unforgivable Sin of Divorce

in Spirit and in truth. But what I now discovered, after twelve years of fasting, was the heart and purpose of God for fasting toward *"the least of these."*

Isaiah 58:6-12 Revisited

Isaiah Chapter 58 is the great Old Testament fasting passage that sets the "high water mark" for Old Testament teaching on the spiritual discipline of fasting. Arthur Wallis named his classic book on fasting, *God's Chosen Fast*, after this passage. I had read and studied these verses many times over the years. I had even written a devotional on this passage for my devotional book on fasting. But this time was different. This time I saw what I hadn't seen before.

The people of God in Isaiah's day were not very different from the people of God in our day. They were an outwardly religious people who knew how to go through all of the right

> *"In the midst of their religious fasting, they needed a spiritual reality check."*

religious motions. They knew both the vocabulary and the expectations of their religion-shaped spirituality, including fasting. Like many believers today, they fasted, but often for the wrong reasons. Outwardly they gave every appearance of desiring to know God and His ways, delighting in the "nearness of God" (Isaiah 58:2). But when they fasted nothing happened, and they had slowly become aware of this unsettling reality: *"Why have we fasted, and you see it not? Why have we humbled ourselves, and you take no knowledge of it?"* (58:3)

The Least Of These

In the midst of their religious fasting, they needed a spiritual reality check. God's response to their dilemma, delivered through Isaiah, was simple yet profound. All of their fasting, He told them, was little more than outward religious show. When they fasted it was all about themselves. They were willing to fast and look religious on the one hand while abusing their workers on the other, without ever grasping the hypocrisy of their actions. The genuine humility of fasting had given way to the false humility of a religion-shaped spirituality and its outward religious "show," devoid of any spiritual power.

The God of Abraham, Isaac and Jacob wanted His people to do the right thing for the right reasons. So, through Isaiah, God highlighted the hypocrisy of their behavior and

> *"Genuine spiritual freedom is a faith and a fasting which manifests itself in good deeds."*

proceeded to explain what true fasting is really all about. True fasting is about breaking yokes of bondage and bringing people into genuine freedom, a genuine spiritual freedom with practical consequences. It's a spiritual freedom that expresses itself in practical ways by reaching out to the hungry, the homeless and the naked. Genuine spiritual freedom is a faith and a fasting which manifests itself in good deeds. Now if any of this sounds vaguely familiar, like reaching out to *"the least of these,"* it should. It's what Jesus would later describe in Matthew 25, demonstrating once again the consistency of the heart of God and of biblical teaching.

Now comes the critical question: When was the last time you

The Unforgivable Sin of Divorce

fasted on behalf of the hungry, the homeless, the naked, the stranger, the prisoner, etc.? There is a profound sense in which genuine, biblical fasting is about others - the least of these - rather than about ourselves.

The Blessings of Fasting God's Way

Now, if everything we have just seen and read isn't enough conviction for one day, notice what God says will be the result of such fasting (Isaiah 58:8ff): *"If you remove the yoke from your midst, The pointing of the finger, and speaking wickedness, And if you give yourself to the hungry, And satisfy the desire of the afflicted"*:

1. Your light will break out like the dawn,
2. Your recovery will speedily spring forth;
3. Your righteousness will go before you;
4. The glory of the Lord will be your rear guard;
5. You will call, and the Lord will answer; You will cry, and He will say, 'Here I am';
6. Your light will rise in darkness;
7. Your gloom will become like mid-day;
8. The Lord will a) continually guide you, b) satisfy your desire in scorched places, c) give strength to your bones;
9. You will be like a watered garden, and like a spring of water whose waters do not fail;
10. Those from among you will rebuild the ancient ruins;
11. You will raise up the age-old foundations;
12. You will be called the repairer of the breach, the restorer of the streets in which to dwell.

The Least Of These

There is a spiritual truth in the statement that God blesses His people simply because they are His people. As Paul says, we have been blessed with every spiritual blessing in heavenly places. But it is also true (which means that it is a "paradox" - two truths held in tension) that there are times and circumstances when God's blessing is "conditioned" upon our obedience - such as fasting for the right reasons. Do you want the blessings described in this passage? Do you want to be known as *"the repairer of the breach"* and *"the restorer of the streets in which to dwell"*? Well, you won't achieve these by acting religious inside the four walls of a Church. That didn't work for ancient Israel. Why do we think it will work for us? No. The pathway to the blessings God promises here in Isaiah 48 passes through

> *"There is a spiritual truth in the statement that God blesses His people simply because they are His people."*

genuine humility, genuine fasting and earnest seeking after God on behalf of the hungry, the homeless, the naked, the dispossessed, the stranger, the prisoner and all those people who collectively make up *"the least of these."*

The "Unforgivable Sin of Divorce"

And this leads to my final thought on *"the unforgivable sin of divorce."* To put it simply, the evangelical church in America has committed what I am slowly coming to regard as *"the unforgivable sin of divorce"* - we have divorced the Message of the Kingdom from the Work of the Kingdom. And we have done this with disastrous consequences.

The Unforgivable Sin of Divorce

When viewed from within a cultural context, our Postmodern culture has concluded that it can manifest good deeds without Jesus. The Church has concluded that it can manifest Jesus without good deeds. Our Postmodern culture's plan appears to be working. The Church's plan is a disaster.

On the one hand, we have created a *"message without a model"* which has produced an abstract Christianity often divorced from real people with real problems. We seem to have concluded that our multi-million dollar church campuses, our brilliantly

> *". . . we have divorced the 'Message of the Kingdom' from the 'Work of the Kingdom.' And we have done this with disastrous consequences."*

prepared and eloquently delivered messages, our multimedia presentations and our free lattes will so impress and overwhelm people that they will forget about their hunger, their homelessness, their nakedness, their alienation and everything else they were struggling with in their daily lives. But any such spiritual palliative [39] is at best only temporary.

On the other hand, we have left the *"work of the Kingdom"* up to either para-church or non-church related agencies. By leaving it to para-church agencies we have sent the subtle message that if you really want to do good you'll need to

---

[39] A "palliative" is something that reduces the effects or symptoms of a medical condition without curing it; or something that is intended to make a bad situation seem better but that does not really improve the situation.

leave the church in order to do it. And by leaving such things to non-church or community agencies we have fallen victim to a not-so-subtle message that the church is irrelevant to people's needs; therefore, the Kingdom of God is unnecessary, which makes this sin of "divorce" so unforgivable.

Reflections For A Jesus-Shaped Spirituality

I believe that it is the heart of God to reconcile this "divorce" and to change this situation. For several years now I have been hearing the Holy Spirit say that God wants His church to take the Kingdom of God *"back to the streets."* And I believe that the organic house church movement will have a vital role to play in taking both the Message of the Kingdom and the Work of the Kingdom back into our homes and our neighborhoods through an emphasis upon good deeds.

Reflection Question # 1 - What did you learn from this passage in Isaiah 58 that you did not know before? How has what you have learned affected your understanding of fasting and good deeds?

Reflection Question # 2 - When was the last time you fasted (went without food) on behalf of the *"the least of these"* in your community? Consider the following:

✎   Set aside a day to fast on behalf of *"the least of these"* in your community.

The Unforgivable Sin of Divorce

✎ Take the money you would have spent on food during that fasting time and donate it to a local homeless shelter, or use it to buy groceries for a family in need, or donate it to a local food bank.

✎ As you fast and pray, use the "Think List" on Page 61 to write down any ideas you have on other good deeds you can do on behalf of *the least of these.*

The Least Of These

Chapter 7

Are Good Deeds Optional?

The issue of the believer and good deeds raises several questions. For example, one of the most frequently asked questions has to do with who should be the object of our good deeds. Shouldn't believers limit (or at least focus) their good deeds to other believers (we addressed this in Chapter 3)? The second frequently asked question is, *"Didn't Jesus say that good deeds, especially to the poor, are optional?"*

Both of these questions recently surfaced within the organic house church community. What caught my attention was a house church manifesto written by a good friend and house church leader in which he argued that serving the poor is NOT a primary function of the Church. Instead, he argued, serving the poor (*"the least of these"*) presented a potential distraction which threatened to distract the Church from its primary role of proclaiming the Kingdom of God.

Upon reflection, I believe my friend's argument was essentially three-fold. His *first argument* was unspoken but clearly implied, namely, that good deeds are not integral to either the message or the ministry of the Kingdom of God. In response to this implied argument, I believe what we presented earlier in Chapters 3 and 4 of this book clearly refutes this argument. Both the example of Jesus and the clear teaching of Scripture should leave no doubt that good deeds are indispensable in the Jesus-shaped spirituality of the Kingdom of God.

The Least Of These

My friend's *second argument* focused on the question of who should be the object of the Church's good deeds. And his *third argument* dealt with the idea that good deeds toward others are optional for the Church. These last two arguments are both common and important, so I want to take the time to address each of them.

"These, But Not Those"

In his second argument my friend argued from Matthew 25:31ff that Jesus' admonition to care for *"the least of these"* referred to the Church's responsibility to care for its own. He based his argument on the use of the phrase *"brothers of mine"* in verse 40. According to his argument, Jesus is obviously telling the sheep (i.e., the Church) that they have a responsibility to *"care for their own."*

Now, while we might be tempted to come to this conclusion on a casual reading of the passage, closer examination raises issues which make this conclusion unworkable. For example, if this argument is valid, then who are the goats (verse 45) supposed

"The principle of consistency in biblical interpretation would suggest that both passages should be referring to the same group."

to be caring for? Other goats? The sheep? Who? Is Jesus really arguing that each group is only responsible for caring for its own, with no thought given to anyone else? This interpretation would put Jesus at odds with His own words in Luke 6:32ff that His followers are to love and serve others,

Are Good Deeds Optional?

even their enemies (see our treatment of this passage in Chapter 3). But there's more.

The principle of consistency in biblical interpretation would suggest that both passages should be referring to the same group. To better see this we need to look at these two verses in a side-by-side comparison:

Sheep/Righteous - Matthew 25:40 *"And the King will answer and say to them, 'Truly I say to you, to the extent that you did it to one of these brothers of Mine, even the least of them, you did it to Me.'"*

Goats/Unrighteous - Matthew 25:45 *"Then He will answer them, saying, 'Truly I say to you, to the extent that you did not do it to one of the least of these (inference: "my brothers"), you did not do it to Me.'"*

Now, we should notice that the common denominator between these two verses is the reference to *"the least of these,"* not to brothers which only occurs in one of the passages. And *"the least of these"* are defined in **both** passages, not as brothers but as the hungry, the thirsty, the stranger, the naked, the sick and the prisoner. In these two passages, both the sheep and the goats (believers and unbelievers) are being evaluated by the same standard - how they treated *"the least of these,"* not by how they treat "their own" (i.e., "brothers").

So, what did Jesus mean by *"these brothers of Mine"*? Perhaps Jesus was using the term "brothers" the same way that the Apostle Paul would use the same term some 135

The Least Of These

times in his letters to the Churches. Was Paul only addressing himself to the men of the Church (afer all, he calls them "brothers")? Or did Paul intend for his letters to be read by and apply to just the men in the group, but not the women? Of course not! Paul's use of "brothers" was a rhetorical usage which included everyone in his extended audience. I believe the same is true here. And such an interpretation eliminates perceived inconsistencies in the passage and satisfies the principle of consistency in biblical interpretation.

Christians today seem to have the same problem interpreting the term "brother" as 1st Century Jews had interpreting the term "neighbor" in Luke 10:29ff. When a Jewish expert in the Law asked Jesus *"Who is my neighbor?"* Jesus used the parable of "The Good Samaritan" to illustrate that the Jewish restriction of the term "neighbor" to only fellow Jews was unacceptable to God. Similarly, I believe the attempt to restrictively define the term "brother" in Matthew 25 to only fellow believers represents the same fallacy and is contrary to the teachings of Jesus as we saw earlier in Chapter 3 in our examination of Luke 6:32ff.

"If Versus When"

The third prong of the argument offered by my friend dealt with whether or not serving the poor was an optional function of the church. He based his argument on this passage in Mark:

"But Jesus said, 'Leave her alone. Why do you trouble her? She has done a beautiful thing to me. For you always have

Are Good Deeds Optional?

the poor with you, and whenever you want, you can do good for them. But you will not always have me.'" (Mark 14:6-7)

His argument went like this (quote):

"Jesus clearly said that seeking the Kingdom and staying within his righteous laws is our main priority. It's foundational and compulsory. Compared to this it is voluntary – and not compulsory – to help the poor. Jesus said it like this: "The poor you will always have with you (which means we will never eliminate poverty, even if we want to), and you can help them if you want" (Mk 14:7). Jesus knew that his followers, having their goals confused, will forever become busy solving the never-ending problems of the world and will not have time for their original mission: to expand the rule of God over as many people and people groups as possible."

I believe there are several problems with this interpretation. *First*, according to this argument, Jesus told the disciples that ministering to the poor was something they could do *"if they wanted to."* The problem here is that this isn't what the passage says, as we can see from our quotation of the verse above. The Greek term involved, and erroneously interpreted by my friend to mean "if," is the Greek word *hotan*, an "adverb of time" meaning "whenever" and used of events which are

"If ministering good deeds to 'the least of these' is optional and conditional for the believer (in other words, you can do it 'if you want to'), then so is prayer."

The Least Of These

likely to occur. [40] In other words, "when" as opposed to "if." The same word is used by Jesus in His instructions to the disciples concerning prayer in Matthew Chapter 6:

*"And **when** you pray, you must not be like the hypocrites. For they love to stand and pray in the synagogues and at the street corners, that they may be seen by others. Truly, I say to you, they have received their reward. But **when** you pray, go into your room and shut the door and pray to your Father who is in secret. And your Father who sees in secret will reward you."* (Matthew 6:5-6).

Let's be clear on this point. If ministering good deeds to *"the least of these"* is optional and conditional for the believer (in other words, you can do it *"if you want to"*), then so is prayer. It's that simple, and that profound.

This raises my **second** problem with my friend's interpretation that Jesus was establishing priorities. Here's what he said:

"Jesus clearly said that seeking the Kingdom and staying within his righteous laws is our main priority. It's foundational and compulsory."

Now, this is more complicated than it looks. Why? Because I do believe that Jesus sets priorities. But Jesus' argument in Mark 14:6-7 has to do with timing as opposed to priorities. Jesus was preparing the disciples for His approaching

---

[40]See Liddell and Scott, *A Greek-English Lexicon*, page 1264.

Are Good Deeds Optional?

departure. Time was short. He would soon be gone. Their time together was important and He would soon be gone. So Jesus tells the disciples, *"the poor you always have with you . . . . but you do not always have Me."* In other words, *"the poor will be here after I am gone. Then you can help them. But not right now."*

Is serving the poor a priority for the Kingdom of God? I believe we have already demonstrated in this book that the scriptural answer is "yes." But on this particular day in the life of Jesus and His disciples, it wasn't timely. Serving the poor

> *"This wasn't a lecture on the difference between compulsory things and voluntary things. This was a practical lesson about timing."*

could wait a little while. On this particular day it was time for the disciples to focus their time and attention on Jesus, to anoint Him for His upcoming departure (Mark 14:8) and to spend what little time was left to them on ministering to Him. This wasn't a lecture on the difference between compulsory things and voluntary things. This was a practical lesson about timing.

In addition to the two primary issues I have already raised and treated concerning my friend's understanding of the biblical attitude toward *"the least of these,"* I have some additional concerns. For example, the argument offered up that serving *"the least of these"* is optional, or voluntary, rather than compulsory could be consistently applied to serving poor Christians. If, as he argues, seeking the Kingdom is our main priority and serving the poor is a potential distraction, then shouldn't this rule apply across the

The Least Of These

board? It doesn't take any less time or any fewer resources to serve the poor Christians in our midst. Indeed, this seemed to be the issue in Acts Chapter 6. There the church had to find an arrangement which released the Apostolic leadership to devote themselves to one aspect of Kingdom ministry, while at the same time appointing and empowering other disciples to serve the practical needs of *"the least of these"* in their midst. It wasn't an "either/or" choice. They understood the need for "both/and" as well as the need for delegation among the various gifts.

Finally, my friend argues that *"Jesus knew that his followers, having their goals confused, will forever become busy solving the never-ending problems of the world and will not have time for their original mission: to expand the rule of God over as many people and people groups as possible."*

Let's examine this for just a moment. Of the more than 1,000 mission plans to fulfill the Great Commission which the Church launched in the thirty years between 1970 and 2000, none succeeded by increasing the number of Christians as an overall percentage of the world's population (in fact, the actual percentage declined from 33.4% in 1970 to 33.0% in the year 2000). If we are going to argue that service to *"the least of these"* is optional because they will always be with us, then we might as well give up on evangelism, too. We don't seem to be reducing the percentage of "the lost" (or increasing the percentage of believers) any more quickly or significantly than we are reducing the number of "the poor."

Furthermore, the "either/or" perspective advocated by many evangelical leaders (in other words, my friend isn't alone in this belief) fails to take into consideration the very real

Are Good Deeds Optional?

possibility that God's plan for expanding His Kingdom (His rule over the lives of as many people as possible) just may include using our self-sacrificial service to *"the least of these"* as one of His key tools for accomplishing His Kingdom goals.

Let's be clear. Those who use this passage to argue that, because Jesus said the poor will always be with us, this means you can never eliminate poverty, so don't bother even trying, are offering up a red herring argument that completely misses the point. Biblically speaking, I do not believe it is the calling of the Church

> *"God's plan for expanding His Kingdom just may include using our self-sacrificial service to 'the least of these' as one of His key tools for accomplishing His Kingdom goals."*

to eliminate poverty or to establish the Kingdom of God by eliminating social injustice. No. Rather, I believe that it is the call of each individual believer (and of the Church as a corporate body) to match their message of the Kingdom with good deeds which model and demonstrate God's redemptive love toward people. In short, I reject the social agenda of the world and embrace the Kingdom agenda of the Lord Jesus Christ.

Which Commission?

In his book, *The Faith*, Chuck Colson (whom I greatly admired) argued that Christians have a Cultural Commission comparable to The Great Commission. According to Colson,

The Least Of These

believers have been given a Cultural Commission by Scripture to transform our culture. I disagree. I do not find any Cultural Commission in Scripture (no, not even in Genesis Chapter 9). But I do find two related things.

First, I do find *"Cultural Consequences."* What I mean is this; in both Scripture and history, the Kingdom of God has consequences. Redeemed people tend to dramatically impact the world in which they live. A redeemed John Newton abandoned the slave trade which had been his life, and devoted himself to the proclamation of the gospel. As a consequence of Newton's redeemed life he offered spiritual encouragement to a redeemed member of Parliament named William Wilberforce, who in turn devoted himself to the abolition of the slave trade. Those are the *"Cultural Consequences"* of the Kingdom of God. And how many people through the centuries have come to faith as the result of being touched or impacted by such *"Cultural Consequences"* of such redeemed individuals.

> *". . . in both Scripture and history, the Kingdom of God has consequences. Redeemed people tend to dramatically impact the world in which they live."*

Second, I also find a *"Compassion Commission"* given by Jesus Himself in Matthew 25 to those who would be called by His name and who would seek to live out a Jesus-shaped spirituality. Historically, I see that *"Compassion Commission"* continually worked out in the on-going life of the Church.

Are Good Deeds Optional?

Weeping For Our Generation

If I had to choose one word to describe Western Christianity I think I would choose the word "superficial." Western Christianity seems to be a mile wide and an inch deep (and shrinking in both directions). We excel in offering simplistic answers to complex questions. We have traded theology for therapy, self-denial for self-indulgent prosperity, sacrificial worship for contemporary worship, and many other trade-offs which have left the Church spiritually impoverished. We no longer cultivate tall theological trees with deep roots which draw on ancient wells of time-proven truths. Instead, we sip our spirituality from dixie cups, offering little more than over-sweetened Kool-Aid to a Postmodern culture that looks at us in disbelief as they openly wonder, *"Is this all you have?"*

> *". . . we sip our spirituality from dixie cups, offering little more than over-sweetened Kool-Aid to a Postmodern culture that looks at us in disbelief as they openly wonder, 'Is this all you have?'"*

Historically, few things drive the roots of the church deeper than its willingness to weep on behalf of others. Writing in *Christianity Today Online*, John Fischer suggests that greatest legacy left to the Church of our generation by the late Dr. Francis A. Schaeffer may have been his ability and willingness to weep for a lost culture,

"But perhaps, in the end, his greatest influence on the church will not be his words as much as his tears. The same

The Least Of These

things that made Francis Schaeffer cry in his day should make us cry in ours." [41]

I agree with Fischer and believe it is time for us to once again discover what it means to weep for our generation. We need more theologians who have "skin in the game," who don't practice the art of theology from academic ivory towers, or from basements with

> *"We need weeping theologians who combine the art of theology with incarnational living among 'the least of these.'"*

nothing more than an internet connection and a flashy website. Rather, in obedience to the *"Compassion Commission"* of Jesus, we need weeping theologians who combine the art of theology with incarnational living among *"the least of these."* Until you as a theologian have wept the tears of the broken-hearted, then you have not yet touched the heart of God in your theology. Don't believe me? Just ask Jeremiah. Or better yet, ask Jesus who wept over Jerusalem and over Lazarus and probably over others we will never know about.

Personally, I find it most ironic that in my own life God had me write a book opposing Universal Salvation and defending the traditional (i.e., Biblical) understanding of conscious eternal punishment, while at the same time leading a food rescue ministry and serving in a men's shelter. I call it

[41]John Fischer, *"Learning to Cry for the Culture: Let's remember Francis Schaeffer's most crucial legacy--tears"* in Christianity Today Online, posted 3/19/2007 09:23AM

Are Good Deeds Optional?

"theology encounters reality," the art of incarnationally living out what we profess to believe and learning to weep for our generation in the process.

Reflections For A Jesus-Shaped Spirituality

For those of us seeking to authentically live out a Jesus-shaped spirituality of good deeds toward *"the least of these,"* it is not our goal or desire to impress anyone. Rather, secure in the knowledge that we perform for an Audience of One, we walk in the simple obedience of a Jesus-shaped spirituality while praying that the "Julians" of this world might one day take notice that *"The impious Galileans support not only their poor, but ours as well."* [42]

Reflection Question # 1 - What did you learn from this Chapter about good deeds that you did not know before?

Reflection Question # 2 - What would you say to someone who argued that believers are supposed to limit their good deeds to other believers?

Reflection Question # 3 - What would you say to someone who argued that good deeds toward *"the least of these"* are optional in the life of the believer?

---

[42]Gerald Sittser's, ***Water From A Deep Well: Christian Spirituality From Early Martyrs To Modern Missionaries***, (Downers Grove: IVP Books, 2007), page 56.

The Least Of These

Chapter 8

Good Deeds In "Felony Flats"

Perhaps you have read or heard Mark Twain's account of his move to Carson City, Nevada in the mid-1800s. According to Twain he had never seen such a wretched hive of sin, corruption and villainy. *"I concluded that it was no place for a Presbyterian, and I did not remain one for very long."* Mark Twain would have felt right at home in the West Central neighborhood of Spokane.

At the time of our ministry there, the West Central Neighborhood of Spokane was the second poorest neighborhood in the state of Washington. It was known throughout the city as "felony flats." Due to it's proximity to the local jail, over the years it had become the "containment zone" for gangs, ex-felons, parolees, sex offenders, drug-related crime, domestic violence, and the impoverished and the dispossessed of the city. Generations of dysfunctional behavior had raised up successive generations of families for whom drugs, domestic violence and poverty were a way of life. A handful of traditional churches had struggled for years to establish a foothold for the Kingdom of God with only marginal success. Feasibility studies conducted by church planting organizations over the years concluded that planting a successful new work was simply not feasible or recommended. In the words of Mark Twain, it was no place for a Presbyterian. But then, God does love a challenge.

The Least Of These

A Man of Peace Named Larry

Into this rich soil of hopelessness and despair God planted a man of peace named Larry Whiston. Larry had recently spent six years in prison for a crime of violence. In the depth of his own personal prison of despair and hopelessness, God had touched Larry's life, transformed it and turned him into a man of faith and of peace. Upon his release from prison Larry lived for two years at the local Union Gospel Mission while participating in the Mission's various rehabilitation programs. Afterwards he moved into a small duplex in the West Central neighborhood on West Broadway. With help from Christian friends, Larry began reaching out to his new neighbors and offering a weekly Bible study. The Bible study quickly grew until it filled the small apartment. A meal was added and the outreach became an evening of food and fellowship. In the Spring, as weather permitted, the meal and study moved outside under white pavilion tents in the front yard where more people from the neighborhood could attend. By mid-summer it had grown into a weekly neighborhood barbecue and Bible study with nearly 100 people attending every Monday night.

On Any Given Monday

By Spring of the following year, the Off Broadway Family Outreach (as it was now officially known), represented a coalition of people and ministries who had come together to partner with Larry to see the West Central neighborhood spiritually touched by the power of the gospel and the practical outworking of the Kingdom of God. This amazing story of kingdom ministry was on full display every Monday

Good Deeds In "Felony Flats"

evening throughout that Summer (which is when I became involved)at W. 1817 Gardner in the heart of West Central. Larry had become a Luke 10 Person of Peace in West Central, and Larry's front yard was ministry central every Monday.[43]

A typical Monday would begin as early as 8AM as Larry Whiston, Jan Foland and I would begin our rounds to pick up food from the Union Gospel Mission, Tidymans, Safeway and other local stores which donated food items to the outreach. By early afternoon volunteers would begin arriving at Larry's house as white pavilion tents went up, the signal to the neighborhood that Monday night had arrived. Food for the evening meal was already being assembled in the Kitchen. Volunteers would fan out through the neighborhood, handing out flyers to remind residents that tonight was the night for food and fellowship. Passing cars would stop long enough for someone to ask what time dinner will be served. *"Six o'clock!"* was the reply as the car moved on.

By 4 o'clock people would begin arriving and visiting among themselves. The evening music team would arrive and begin setting up their equipment and tuning their instruments. Volunteers scurry around setting up chairs (there are always more people than chairs), but before the evening is over it would be standing room only. More people would arrive. Jan Foland, then an art teacher from Salk Middle School would arrive bringing ice, punch, desserts, and more people. Soon she would be busy getting the evening's children's lesson

---

[43]In the interest of "full disclosure" I was an elder/director in The Off-Broadway Family Outreach from 2004 through 2006 and personally participated in the events described in what follows.

The Least Of These

ready. Neighborhood kids flocked around Jan like bees around honey! Soon Larry would arrive bringing another car load of people from outside the immediate neighborhood. People from other parts of the city would catch the city bus and travel to be there. The evening was already hectic and it hadn't officially begun yet! Gale Smith and Kitty Shipley would be busy overseeing food preparation in the kitchen. I would teach the evening lesson out of the Gospel of John, but in the mean time my extensive seminary training was needed at the grill - barbecuing hot dogs for the evening meal. More people arrived including volunteer help from various local area churches.

By 6 o'clock you would think that someone had rung a dinner bell. People came from all over the neighborhood for a dinner of hot dogs, chili, chips, salads and dessert. By 6:30 there would be 200 or more people crowded into Larry's 40' X 30' front yard, spilling onto the sidewalk and into the street. On a humorous note, one evening when we had well over 300 people milling around, someone called the police about a "drunk and disorderly" person who stumbled in. The first squad car arrived, took one look around and called for "back up." Eventually there were four squad cars and a bunch of very nervous officers until we could reassure them that this wasn't a riot in the making - just a church potluck!

Over the more relaxed atmosphere of dinner - served in the front yard on paper plates around makeshift tables - people would open up about their struggles. Addiction to drugs and alcohol, struggles with domestic violence, poverty, drug deals in their front yards at night accompanied by gun shots in the dark. The list of struggles and needs seemed endless. I had a lengthy conversation with "Nick" a gay man in his late 20s who had been ostracized by his Christian family. Here, on this evening, in a non-threatening environment Nick freely told his story of struggle, pain and rejection. Nick and I would have several such conversations over the course of that Summer. What Nick knew was that, around us, he was loved.

By 7 o'clock nearly everyone had something to eat. But the kitchen would remain open as long as anyone was hungry and asked for something to eat. Our dinner rule was simple, *"No one leaves hungry."* There was also free bread (compliments of local super markets) for people to take home. Shortly after 7PM the music team would hand out home-made songbooks and the worship time would begin with numerous praise and worship songs. Around 7:30 the worship would wind down. Larry would take the microphone to share his amazing testimony (there were always new people who hadn't heard it yet).

I followed Larry and invited people to share what God had been doing in their lives over the past week. In a sea of hopelessness and need, there were always testimonies of God's goodness and faithfulness. For several weeks I shared from the Gospel of John about *"Seven Reasons To Believe"* based upon the seven great signs of John's Gospel. My message was simple: *"God cares about the circumstances and situations of your life, and He has the power to transform whatever you are going through."* It was a message that resonated with the crowd.

After 20 minutes of interactive teaching with the crowd I would ask everyone to break into smaller groups to talk about what they were learning and to pray for each other. That was when the serious work of the evening began as people opened up in these small groups, sharing their struggles and asking for prayer. There was prayer, weeping and rejoicing. And for a few hours that evening, the cloud of hopelessness and despair which seemed to hang over this neighborhood like a perpetual fog, was broken as the Presence of God settled over the people gathered in the front yard of W. 1817 Gardner on that summer evening. Somewhere around 8:30 PM the evening would begin to wind down of its own accord. People would begin leaving, while others would remain to talk, to ask for prayer or to simply "linger" a while longer. Volunteers would begin the process of "tear down," stacking chairs, folding tents, collecting garbage and cleaning the kitchen. Although the evening was officially over, people remained standing on the sidewalk, talking about what had transpired that evening. God had been good, and a small foothold for the Kingdom of God was established in the West Central neighborhood of Spokane, Washington.

Baptisms In West Central

On one Monday evening we had the thrill of baptizing several neighborhood people who had made new or renewed professions of faith, or who had professed Christ previously but had never been baptized. We set up a wading pool in the front yard and people gathered from around the neighborhood to witness the event! I spoke briefly from Romans 10:9, *"if you confess with your mouth Jesus as Lord, and believe in your heart that God raised Him from the dead, you shall be saved."* The neighborhood had the opportunity to hear the gospel and an explanation of the meaning of believer's baptism. Larry Whiston and I baptized several people, as did other volunteers who baptized several

Good Deeds In "Felony Flats"

neighborhood people they had been working with and praying for. The events of that evening resonated for weeks through a neighborhood which thought it had "seen everything"!

Reaching Out With Back Packs And School Supplies

From its beginning The Off Broadway Family Outreach had a large children's ministry. Kids from all over the neighborhood would show up on any given Monday night (50 to 75 kids was normal for a Monday night). For many of these kids Monday night represented the day's only hot meal, or an island of tranquility in a very un-tranquil neighborhood or home setting. Many of these kids attended the local elementary school where the poverty rate among the students and their families ran as high as 92%. As a result, many of these kids could not afford the normal school supplies which most of us take for granted.

One of our children's workers had the idea of providing back packs and school supplies for all of the kids involved in our ministry (this was before back pack and school supply drives were as common as they are today). After soliciting the help of community organizations and businesses, including the local Campfire Girls, WalMart and Costco to name a few, we were able to hand out 40 back packs to our ministry kids on the Monday night before school began.

But the need kept growing, and so did the vision. So the children's' ministry team rounded up another 60 back packs which they delivered to Holmes Elementary school on the following Friday, leaving it up to the staff of the school to decide who would receive them). The Principle was moved and told our team that no one had ever done that for them before. By the end of September we had handed out a total of 150 back packs to local neighborhood school kids.

Drugs And Amazing Grace

It is no secret that drugs were and are a plague in the West Central neighborhood. The drug traffic feeds a seemingly endless cycle of property crime, counterfeiting, domestic violence, poverty, and the cycle goes on. Is there any hope of breaking this cycle? Yes! All you need to do is be willing to leave your comfortable church box, stand outside the doors of known drug dealers, pray for them and sing "Amazing Grace." And therein lies a story.

One evening during that summer our leadership team felt compelled to go to a local known drug house at 10PM after our weekly leadership meeting. We stood on the sidewalk outside of the apartment where a known drug dealer lived and trafficked. There we prayed and ended by singing "Amazing Grace." It wasn't until several weeks later that we learned "the rest of the story."

Unknown to us, inside of the apartment was a drug dealer whose parents had been ministers in a church. This person had been raised in a church home, but had begun walking in open rebellion against God after the death of her parents. When we sang "Amazing Grace" it became too much and she "lost it." Something broke inside this person, who realized the depths to which she had fallen. A series of events followed over the course of a few weeks, including a

Good Deeds In "Felony Flats"

police raid and the issuing of a warrant for her arrest. In early September this drug dealer came to our ministry house and told us the whole story. She broke down and said she wanted to get out of this lifestyle and to turn herself in to the authorities. Larry Whiston, our team leader, looked this person in the eyes and said, *"We love you, and we will walk with you through this."* Personal redemption often begins with a decision followed by a journey.

Requiem For A Drug Dealer

When your neighborhood becomes your ministry family you eventually become a part of the family crises which occur within the neighborhood. That's what happened when Sonny died. As a young black man Sonny had served two tours in Vietnam. When he left the military he joined the railroad as a brakeman/conductor where he worked for another 15 years while raising his family. After retiring from the railroad his life took several turns, which eventually led him into the drug trade in the West Central neighborhood.

When Off Broadway began its outreach on Gardner, Sonny lived in an apartment directly across the street from our ministry house. We soon befriended one another and Sonny became a frequent visitor at our Monday night meetings. Sonny would also come to visit with Larry late at night and discuss what God was doing in his life. He would even bring some of his "troubled" clients over to talk with Larry about how to break free from the drug lifestyle (something much harder to do than most Christians realize). Sonny had made a profession of faith as a young man. Now, over the course of that Summer he began to see the neighborhood change

The Least Of These

as the result of God working through our ministry there. Drug houses were closing up, drug cartels were being broken and drug users and dealers were coming to know the Lord. Sonny began to realize and talk openly about his own need to change his life, to renew his commitment to Christ, and to break free from the drug lifestyle which had engulfed him.

In early January of 2005 Sonny entered the hospital to be treated for pneumonia. The treatment was successful, but on Sunday he experienced a seizure. The doctors worked to save him, but he suffered a heart attack and died, all within the span of a few minutes. He thought he would be going home the following day, but Sonny didn't realize which home he was being called to. But he had made a renewed profession of faith and was drug free when he died.

Sonny's family asked us to do his memorial service. He was part of our neighborhood family, and we agreed. We also insisted on hosting a reception at our ministry house following the service (we also raised money to buy flowers for the funeral). Sonny's funeral was quite an event. Over 150 people attended. Many people, both family and friends, shared testimonies of how Sonny's life had changed. Larry Whiston and I officiated the service, and took the opportunity to share the gospel with the crowd. Later, many of these people came over to our ministry house for the reception. It was packed "wall-to-wall" for two hours with friends and family. Many of them talked openly with us about their own lives and struggles. An example of just one conversation was a young girl who shared with us that the fact that Sonny had broken free of drugs and found Jesus before he died had given her hope of breaking free, too.

Good Deeds In "Felony Flats"

The funeral and reception had a profound impact upon the neighborhood where everyone knew Sonny. It opened several additional ministry doors. Several people who attended the funeral or reception asked us to start Bible studies in their homes and began asking spiritual questions which they had never dared to ask before. The family was deeply touched by all we did for them. And all of this took place because, by God's grace, people just like you reached out with love and good deeds to a neighborhood in need.

Reflections For A Jesus-Shaped Spirituality

Reflection Question # 1 - What about this story had the greatest impact on you? Why?

Reflection Question # 2 - How has this story stimulated your own thinking about possible neighborhood outreach in your own community?

The Least Of These

Chapter 9

More Stories of Good Deeds

Ivan Illich (1926-2002) was a brilliant thinker and insightful critic of modern culture, society and institutions. Illich was once asked his opinion regarding the most effective way to change society. *"Is it violent revolution or is it gradual reform?"* He gave a careful answer. *"Neither,"* he replied. *"If you want to change society, then you must tell an alternative story."*

If we truly want to see both individual believers and Churches change their thinking concerning the importance of good deeds and their role in a Jesus-shaped spirituality, then - as Ivan Illich observed - we need to tell an "alternative story." Hopefully, by this point in this book we have laid the practical and biblical groundwork for that "alternative story." Now, in the remainder of this chapter I want to help tell that story by sharing several stories of good deeds which I have either personally witnessed, or which have come to my attention over the past several years. All of the stories related here involve people just like you. In other words, they were no more qualified than you are to do what they did. They simply stepped out in obedience to what they understood to be the call of God to *"greater love and good deeds."* These are some of their stories.

The Least Of These

Good Deeds With Hollandaise Sauce

Several years ago I was invited to attend a meeting for an upstart coalition of local ministries and organizations which feed free meals to those in need throughout our city. It was sponsored by a local community service organization (Spokane Neighborhood Action Programs), and was led by an AmeriCor/VISTA worker named Gregory Edwards (who is now Father Gregory Edwards of the Orthodox Church). Although I had been involved in feeding as many as 300 people once a week in the poorest neighborhood of our city, I felt like an amateur among pros. The purpose of the meeting was to consider forming a coalition to combine efforts in finding new sources of food for our various feeding programs. In the course of the meeting I made a few suggestions about approaching businesses to help out, including approaching local area restaurants about donating surplus food that might otherwise be thrown away.

After the meeting Gregory Edwards came up to me and asked if I would like to serve on the leadership committee. For reasons I couldn't explain at the time, I accepted and began a journey that quickly became incarnational for me. In a matter of a few weeks, Feed Spokane, a non-profit "food rescue" organization was born. The goal was simple: to find more sources of quality food to place into the shelters, kitchens, ministries and organizations which served both the homeless and others in need.

Over the next five years, during which I served as the unpaid Executive Director, God gave us amazing favor. My artistically gifted wife (a talented graphics designer) donated

More Stories of Good Deeds

her time and talent by designing the logo. As our work became known, the local community responded generously. We built strategic partnerships with the Spokane Chapter of the Washington Restaurant Association and the local health department. Restauranteurs stepped up to donate food, including the owner of the local "Arby's" restaurants. Some 25 area restaurants had become involved when I left after five years. A local business (a brewery, to be exact!) donated a used refrigerated truck for pick ups and deliveries. Five time times we were featured on the front page of the local newspaper. We raised both the quantity and the quality of food served to those in need, and provided some 45,000 pounds of food per year (about 30,000 meals) to some 25 participating agencies.

One of the restaurants to sign on early with Feed Spokane was the finest 5-Star hotel in the city. I would pick up from them at least once per week and the left over food they gave us included such things as prime rib, salmon, basil cream chicken and more.

"When it comes to telling stories about the Kingdom of God, you get more mileage out of prime rib than you do hot dogs."

Finally, the temptation to do something special for a local men's shelter became irresistible. When another large pan of prime rib came through I grabbed it, along with a pan of seafood and a few

The Least Of These

other items. That Thursday night, instead of chili dogs, I served the 30 men at the shelter prime rib, mashed potatoes, vegetables, croissants and chilled shrimp/prawns. Homeless men accustomed to Ramen Noodles stared at their plates in disbelief. Marty, the shelter director and a good friend, joked with the men, *"I don't eat this good at home!"* It was a great evening, and the men joked about it for weeks afterwards. When it comes to telling stories about the Kingdom of God, you get more mileage out of prime rib than you do hot dogs. And I have a basic rule. If I wouldn't serve it to Jesus or my own family, why would I serve it to *"the least of these"* whom He has called me to love and serve in His name?[44]

Ecumenical Good Deeds

I wish you could meet my friend Rick. I met Rick several years ago when my wife and I were beginning our ministry work with the Off Broadway Family Outreach in the West Central neighborhood of Spokane (see Chapter 8, *"Good Deeds In Felony Flats"*). Working long hours and "full tilt" when most men his age would be enjoying retirement, Rick owns and operates several successful businesses in our community. I was introduced to him as someone who might be interested in helping out financially with our work. When I dropped by to introduce myself and visit with him it was immediately apparent that we had an "ecumenical" issue between us. I was an evangelical Protestant and he was a strong Catholic. After exploring our differences for a while, Rick paused. *"People just need Jesus,"* he said. *"I agree,"*

---

[44]You can learn more about the current work of Feed Spokane on their website: http://www.feedspokane.com.

came my response. And that became the basis for an on-going working relationship focused upon serving *"the least of these."*

On more than one occasion (on numerous occasions, as a matter of fact), I would show up at Rick's primary business on a Monday morning and say, *"Rick, I'm going to have a couple hundred people to feed tonight and I need help buying food."* We would talk about what we were doing in the neighborhood outreach and then Rick would turn to his assistant and say, *"Cut Maurice a check for what he needs."*

Over the next several years Rick became a generous supporter of our work. But his good deeds went beyond simply giving money. When a local shelter for homeless men needed extensive street excavation work for new water and sewer connections in order to open for business, I made the need known and Rick quietly arranged for the work to be done through one of his family's construction businesses. The shelter avoided a large out-of-pocket expense and was able to open on time. When Rick began construction on a new building for one of his businesses he asked me if I knew of any able bodied men at the shelter who needed work. Rick is a big believer in helping homeless men get back to work, get on their feet and begin taking responsibility for their lives. I was able to send him three men whom he successfully employed. They, in turn, were able to get on their feet, out of the shelter and into their own places.

On another visit with Rick and his assistant, Brenda, I told them I might be referring some friends of mine who were leading a new ministry on the streets of our city and needed some encouragement. I passed Rick's contact information on

The Least Of These

to my friends and went on about my various projects.[45] On a subsequent visit to Rick's office I heard the rest of the story. My friends had indeed contacted Brenda, shared their needs concerning an upcoming outreach, and had quickly found a receptive heart. In addition to Rick's substantial help (which I suspected would happen), Brenda was so moved by what they were doing that she, too, decided to get personally involved. She began collecting socks, coats, toiletries and other assorted items. On my next visit, Brenda showed me a back hallway in Rick's office building which she had begun filling up with large bags of donated items she had collected for the upcoming outreach. When my friends shared their desire to provide sack lunches to all of the street people who would be coming to the outreach, Brenda approached a bakery owner in the same building and challenged the owner to donate cookies for the lunches. *"Sure, I can do that,"* came the reply. Funny thing about good deeds. They tend to be contagious. Once you take the lead in doing good, you'll be amazed by who follows.

The Hard Reality of Good Deeds
by Sarah Hennagin

Editor's Note: I met Sarah during my food rescue work with Feed Spokane. Sara would pick up available food for a local ministry which works with homeless street teens in our city. When she offered to write an article about her experience with good deeds I wasn't sure what to expect. What she

---

[45]These friends who needed encouragement in their new ministry were *"Blessings Under The Bridge"*; see their story on page 169.

More Stories of Good Deeds

offered me was an honest "reality check" which illustrates how good deeds are not a quick fix for intractable problems and which explains why my "vacuum cleaner" illustration back in Chapter 2 (page 35) is true more often than most of us would like to believe. All of us who have worked with "the least of these" can relate to Sarah' story. So, my thanks to Sarah for helping all of us to better understand the importance of "persevering" in both love and good deeds.

I have spent nearly seven years now volunteering and eventually working on staff at an organization that serves youth who are homeless and street-involved in downtown Spokane. I've had the joy of doing a lot of the good deeds one would expect, like providing a young person in need with a hot meal, a warm coat, a new pair of socks, a much-needed shower, or a piece of birthday cake. Sometimes I'm not sure how "good" these deeds can be considered, since I am mostly giving away resources that other people have donated. It's quite satisfying to be the person who gets thanked for things that didn't cost me a dime. However, it's sometimes less-than-satisfying to see the same young person the next day . . . day after day . . . and find that the warm coat was stolen by a family member, the socks I gave her are soaking wet and in the trash, or the piece of cake I offered gave him a stomach ache (and now he's grumpy about it). It can get old seeing the same weary faces over and over again and wondering why I should give them one more pair of socks. After a certain point, it can be easy to feel like what I'm doing is not actually helping.

This has been a struggle for many of us who work with my organization (and I'm certain for countless others in similar types of work around the world). I grew up hearing sweet,

The Least Of These

chicken-soup-type stories about one-time acts of charity that changed people's lives forever. Where are all those people, and why don't I know any of them? And why doesn't my nice white pair of socks make a 16-year-old want to stop shooting meth and sleeping outside?

The time I have spent with youth at our organization has been a whole new kind of education for me, with homeless teenagers as my instructors. They have taught me that socks (and all material possessions) are easy-come, easy-go, but real love and people who care are hard things to find. They live in a culture where interest in others is nearly always motivated by self-interest. The unconditional love of Christ and the inherent worth of a human being are foreign concepts, because friends are only worthwhile if they are useful to one's own survival. Love and acceptance are the things they crave most and often the things that most elude them. This really isn't all that different from everyone else in the world; with the youth we serve it's just a lot closer to the surface. Conversations about life and relationships while assisting young ladies in our clothing bank have opened my eyes to the true value of my work, which is more about those conversations than the deodorant and pajama pants I'm helping them find.

In the midst of giving so many other things, I have become convinced that the best thing I can give another person is a little piece of his or her identity. All of us are created in the image of God: *"fearfully and wonderfully made"* (Ps. 139.14). For some people, the way they have grown up and the treatment they have received from others make it very hard for them to see that image in themselves. We have the weighty and beautiful privilege of restoring that image, little

More Stories of Good Deeds

by little, by affirming in others their God-given value. This is no light task, and is not accomplished in a short period of time. Undoing years of abuse and discouragement doesn't happen overnight. It can feel repetitive and hopeless sometimes. We have to choose to "see no one from a human point of view" (2 Cor. 5.16), looking past coping behaviors and layers of protection to see a creation of God seeking love and redemption.

I've had the opportunity to practice this ideal over the last six months or so as I've been getting to know a young woman who started coming to our drop-in center last spring. She just turned 18, and has been addicted to methamphetamine for nearly two years. She alternates between staying at various drug houses and sleeping outside. She comes here to sleep on the couch during the day and to get clothing from our clothing bank, which she excels at leaving in chaotic piles all over our hallway and women's bathroom. It took her more than a month of coming here to have more than a two-word conversation with me. I don't remember exactly how it happened, but somehow I ended up with her one day when she decided she needed to talk to someone about her situation with her boyfriend, which is continually up-and-down. We started to develop some trust, and had more conversations, as well as me occasionally giving her rides to places when she needed it.

Following a chain of circumstances since then, I ended up walking with this young lady through her choice to leave a drug rehab program shortly after entering, and through that experience I realized the heavy load of guilt and pain that many of the youth we see are carrying. It killed me when she said to me, *"I should have known I couldn't do it. I'm just a*

The Least Of These

piece of s*** tweaker anyway." In that moment I realized that despite my frustrations with her erratic behavior and numerous poor choices, my first responsibility is to communicate to her that she is a beautiful, capable young woman who is beloved of Christ and loved by me as well, regardless of her choices and her addiction. I got to tell her as much after she made the above statement to me, and it was enough to make her stop and say, *"Wow. Thank you. That really means a lot."* I think it was a profound moment for her, but it didn't change everything. She still hasn't gone through treatment. She is still on the street, and she still leaves piles of clothing all over our bathroom. But now I do my best to never miss an opportunity to somehow affirm that identity. If nothing else, she knows that I care about her, and perhaps that can be a foundation for things that are a little harder for her to believe.

"Therefore we do not lose heart . . . we fix our eyes not on what is seen, but on what is unseen, since what is seen is temporary, but what is unseen is eternal." (2 Corinthians 4.16,18)

Good Deeds That Change Us

I wish you could meet my friends, Marty and Julie McKinney of Truth Ministries.[46] Marty started out as a hard drinking, Harley-riding rock musician. And he was good at all three! Rock music was his life's passion, and many of the

---

[46]In the interest of full disclosure I should tell you that my wife and I now serve on the Board of Directors of Truth Ministries, thereby providing us with a good excuse to hang out with people we genuinely love! Learn more at http://www.truthministriesspokane.org.

More Stories of Good Deeds

musicians Marty toured with in his early days (who will go unnamed) are well-known and successful musicians today. But God had a different path for Marty and his wife, Julie. Marty left the rock music scene after a life transforming encounter with Jesus. He stopped touring, joined a local church and got a job installing heating and air conditioning systems. But God wasn't done with these two. A still small voice told them that they should be doing more. Finally, they yielded to the voice.

Their spiritual journey soon led them to begin making sandwiches at home and driving downtown at night to distribute them out of the trunk of their car to the homeless. *"We didn't have money or a clue,"* Marty once told me, *"which I suppose makes it real easy to see God at work."*

They were soon surrounded by homeless people in need. And it quickly became apparent that simply handing out sandwiches at night was not enough. They needed to do more. *"Within a few months we were running a make shift, fly-by-night shelter out of at least five different vacant offices,"* Marty recounted. *"We moved probably seven times before we had a permanent building that was up to code and that the city would allow us to operate out of."* That was about the time I first met Marty and Julie on the streets of Spokane. They were literally trying to serve the homeless of the city while staying one step ahead of the Fire Marshall, who seemed intent on putting them out of business. *"Yes, you could say we were smuggling Bibles into Russia, so to speak,"* Marty told me. *"All the religious nuts were sure we were out of God's will because we were technically illegal for the first few months and were literally having to hide."*

The Least Of These

Seven years later, not only has Truth Ministries survived, but it has grown beyond anything Marty and Julie ever imagined possible in the days of handing out sandwiches from the trunk of their car.

"Good deeds done in the name of Jesus change us at least as much as they change the world."

Today, through a series of miraculous provisions, they have their own dedicated building (it even meets code!) where upwards of 40 homeless men receive food and shelter every evening of the year. About a year after moving into the new facility they were contacted by the local ABC-TV affiliate who announced that they wanted to include the shelter in a local *"Extreme Makeover"* by building and donating a kitchen!

When I asked Marty for a story about their amazing journey, he sent me the following. It illustrates what I believe is a genuine biblical reality: Good deeds done in the name of Jesus change us at least as much as they change the world. Here's Marty's story in his own words:

This brings me to tell you one of many beautiful stories of our experiencing God all along the way. My son was 16 at the time we first got started. He was with us while we were handing out sandwiches. He watched as I quit my job of 14 years to do this "crazy thing" and he was there to hear the answering machine at my home when my dad called to tell me I was crazy and to ask what kind of a man would quit his job and jeopardize his family's well being like that. Those were tough times.

About three months after we opened the shelter my son was

More Stories of Good Deeds

working as a volunteer at the shelter during his summer break from school. His shift was on a Saturday, working along side my sister-in-law who also volunteered. My wife and I were at home trying to get some rest.

We had a man in a wheel chair with one leg who was a regular guest at the shelter. He almost always came in drunk and a mess, basically soiling himself and never changing clothes. You can use your imagination on that one and you'll be pretty close. He had been coming in every night for a week, and I would take him into the bathroom, get him into the shower, help him get clean and get him some clean clothes to wear. On this particular Saturday my son was working the check-in desk when this man arrived for the night. So, my son called me:

"Dad? So and So is here."
"Yes?"
"Well, he's here tonight."
"Well son, is he a mess?"
"Yeah Dad, pretty bad."
"Well son, I'm not there. You know what you have to do."
"Yeah Dad, I know," and he hung up the phone.

I'm sure you can imagine the fear of having to be alone with a drunk adult let alone the reality of having to bathe him. My son called back an hour later. This time he talked with my wife,

"Mom, I can't believe how good I feel. I was scared but I knew what I had to do. And after I helped him into the shower he began talking to me. What a great guy! I think I understand God more now. God's so awesome!"

The Least Of These

While he was getting the man dressed my son was looking frantically around the bathroom. The man asked him, *"What are you looking for?"*

"Your other boot!," my son replied.

The man laughed, *"******** I only have one foot!"* That moment became a big joke between the two of them for a long time after that night.

This man began to change, even using a regular bathroom on his own during the day, and sobering up. And he always loved my son for helping him out that one time. They became great friends. A few months later this same man ended up in the I.C.U. at the Hospital. When we went to visit him, there on the wall of his room was his visitor list. All the names were ours: my wife's, my sister's, mine, and at the top, my son. The man died just a couple of weeks later.

My son's contact with someone he would normally avoid, let alone talk to, changed his life forever. His opportunity to serve someone in need gave him a firm foundation and a stronger relationship with the Lord that he will never be able to deny.

The miracle of our work is not the fact that two ordinary people with no money operate a homeless shelter completely on faith and donations. The miracle isn't the fact that many community leaders know

"The real miracle is the reality that, if you're available, God will change your own life in extremes you never imagined possible."

who we are and use our services to give the homeless a place to go. The real miracle is the reality that, if you're available, God will change your own life in extremes you never imagined possible. After 7 years of serving those in need this is just one of thousands of stories that have changed our lives and our relationship with the Lord!

Let's get busy about the Father's business!

Blessings Under The Bridge

I wish you could meet my friends, Mike and Jessica Kovac. Today they have a ministry to *"the least of these"* called *"Blessings Under The Bridge,"* but that wasn't always the case. Just a few years ago they were a working couple whose seventeen year marriage was in shambles. Jessica worked in "high-end" food service at expensive restaurants and Mike had worked at Costco for thirteen years until a back injury led to four botched back surgeries that left him disabled and unable to work. Their marriage was disintegrating into anger, bitterness and emotional alienation when the unexpected happened. Jessica, who had been raised Catholic, had an encounter with the living, risen Jesus which transformed her life. Jessica began reading her Bible and they began attending an evangelical church. She was touched by what the Scriptures had to say about "the poor in spirit" and her thoughts turned to the poor and homeless on the streets of the city. She felt that she was supposed to do something, but what?

At the time, Jessica was working and making good money, so she decided to do something on her own. She decided

The Least Of These

that she would start making good-quality sack lunches and hand them out to homeless people on the streets at night. Mike was skeptical and cynical. *"You're being ridiculous. You're going thru a phase,"* was his response to Jessica's announced plan. People at her church weren't much more helpful, *"You're going to actually touch homeless people?"* was the response of one fellow church-goer.

But Jessica was undeterred. On October 7, 2007 Jessica made her first "foray" into street ministry. *"I attended a Casting Crowns concert that evening,"* she recalled. *"I was dressed to the hilt including high heels."* After the concert, arrayed in her complete evening attire, Jessica drove around downtown Spokane until she spotted a homeless man. She stopped, rolled down the window and asked him if he was hungry. When he answered, *"Yes, I am,"* Jessica handed him a sack lunch. He took the lunch and Jessica watched in stunned amazement as he walked to a nearby dumpster, sat down beside it and proceeded to "inhale" the meal. Jessica was hooked. There would be no turning back now.

After a couple of weeks of doing it alone, Mike agreed to go with her. *"It was bitter cold,"* he told me as he recounted the evening. They spotted an older man pushing his shopping cart containing his worldly possessions up the street. Mike jumped out of the car and offered the man a lunch. *"Why are you doing this?"* the man asked as he accepted the offered meal. At that moment Mike experienced a personal transformation. He went from *"they're all homeless bums who just want money"* to *"if I had a million dollars I'd spend it helping them."*

Now Mike and Jessica were both hooked. Their ministry to

More Stories of Good Deeds

"the least of these" was underway. They met homeless men who slept in the cold on the door steps of local churches. They began handing out blankets in addition to food. One evening in early November, they were serving coffee and sandwiches out of the back of their SUV, parked under a freeway overpass. As it began snowing they were soon surrounded by homeless people. *"It was like we were parked in their living room,"* Mike told me as he related the events of the evening. The needs were irresistible. Mike and Jessica began collecting clothes, shoes (particularly men's size 10 ½), socks (which they learned are like "gold" on the street), personal toiletries and more. People at Jessica's work learned about what she and Mike were doing and began bringing items to give away.

In late November Mike and Jessica had a vision for their first *"Blessings Under The Bridge"* Christmas outreach. They would offer a hot breakfast to the homeless community and they would serve it under the freeway overpass where they had me so many homeless people. They put the outreach together in three weeks and on December 22 they fed over 400 people and handed out gifts of clothes, food and personal toiletries.

It was in these early months of street ministry that Mike and Jessica met Homer. At that time Homer was a homeless alcoholic living beneath the overpass. Mike and Jessica manifested the love of Jesus to Homer and began to work with him to get him off the street and off of alcohol. They eventually helped get him into his own apartment where he could live clean and sober. Jessica also tracked down Homer's family which he had abandoned 28 years earlier and who had been told that Homer was dead. Homer discovered

The Least Of These

that his adult daughter was dying of cystic fibrosis and wanted to be reunited with her dad before she died. In September of 2010 Mike and Jessica went public with Homer's story in the local newspaper.[47] The public responded generously and Mike and Jessica were able to raise enough resources to escort Homer to Florida and to personally reunite Homer with his family who embraced him with open arms. Homer is now clean and sober, off the street and back with family who love him. And Mike and Jessica are moving forward with more *"Blessings Under The Bridge,"* ever conscious of the spiritual truth that *"When you did it to the least of these you did it to me."*

Good Deeds In A Parking Lot

Editor's Note: *This story was sent to me by the Ayre family of Kansas, who receive my semi-regular e-mail newsletter.*

A couple of years ago, my husband was filling a soda machine that sits in front of our business. It was late in the evening when he pulled up and noticed a man sitting in his car in our parking lot. It appeared to him that the man was living in his car because it was filled with all his belongings. He approached him and asked him if he needed help. The man shared how he had lived in Denver but left a few days ago with no where to go and no where to stay. My husband called me and after telling me what this man's situation was

---

[47] *"Man Who Lived under Bridge Plans Reunion with Grown Children,"* The Spokesman-Review, Sept. 9, 2010, posted online at http://www.spokesman.com/stories/2010/sep/09/long-way-from-home/. Learn more about the work of "Blessings Under The Bridge" at http://www.butb.org.

More Stories of Good Deeds

and said, *"Honee, I want to put him up for a couple of nights in a hotel."* I agreed. The man was surprised by our offer yet incredibly thankful! Two days later the man called my husband's cell phone and thanked us again. My husband asked him if he had a job yet and some other living arrangements. He replied, *"No,"* but that he had applied at several fast food restaurants (thinking he could at least eat one meal there while he worked). My husband suggested he come home with him to stay with us until he found a job and got on his feet.

So for a couple of months that summer this man lived in our camper behind our house (which we had just spent all winter fixing up) until he eventually found a job and a place to live. Then we helped him get settled in. Before he left our home he shared that the night he was sitting in his car in our parking lot he had been praying and asking God for help when my husband showed up to fill the soda machine.

I often think how amazing it was that God placed him in our parking lot because our business is located miles from the Interstate and is not the easiest place to find! I sincerely believe God led him right to our parking lot! It was a Jesus experience for me and my family and my son learned the meaning of compassion. Just the week before we met this man my son had asked me, *"Mommy, what is compassion?"* I explained the definition of the word with some examples to help him grasp the meaning, but it wasn't until my husband brought this man home to live with us that he said to his dad, *"Now daddy, that's compassion!"*

Today, Terry (the man I spoke of) is part of our lives. He is now a dear friend who works in our community and

The Least Of These

contributes to the Kingdom of God. He shared with us recently, how he took in a young man who was just released from jail with no where to go, and how he has been ministering to him, not by preaching but by showing him kindness, compassion, and incredible patience because that's what Jesus would do.

Terry seems to always meet people in similar situations to his own, people who are homeless and broke (both financially and spiritually). He tries to help them out with both. He recently met a young couple who have addictions and other problems. He is trying to help while sharing Jesus. He wanted to invite them to a church he has been attending on occasion, but figured they wouldn't come. I suggested to him that he invite them to his apartment and meet there in his own home.

Please pray for Terry's ministry and that God would use this man to reach *the least of these* as you have suggested. I once shared how God values all of us, but He doesn't use us equally. Terry is an example of the man God needs who has made himself valuable to God. And Terry is reaching people my family might not ever meet. I cringe to think how many of *the least of these* would not have met someone like Terry if we had not met him that night in our parking lot and brought him home with us. God does work in mysterious ways!

More Stories of Good Deeds

Reflections For A Jesus-Shaped Spirituality

Reflection Question # 1 - Which of the stories in this section had the greatest impact on you? Why?

Reflection Question # 2 - In the spirit of Ivan Illich, what's your "alternative story" of good deeds? Write out a story of a good deed you have done for someone in need.

Reflection Question # 3 - What can you do to make good deeds an on-going manifestation of your spiritual DNA?

The Least Of These

Chapter 10

Becoming Legendary - Part 1

Allow me to introduce you to a legend, someone of a previous era whose life became legendary for his "good deeds" and his impact for the Kingdom of God.

William Thomas Stead is known throughout schools of journalism around the world as the father of modern investigative journalism. He was also a committed Christian whose life offers us an example of someone committed to good deeds and making a difference for the Kingdom of God.

Born in England in 1849, W. T. Stead was the son of a Congregational minister. Home-schooled by his father, by the age of five he could read both Latin and English. In 1861 Stead was sent to finish his education at a school for boys. While there he had a personal encounter with God. He was deeply touched. His life was set ablaze by the fires of the Second Evangelical Awakening, which had begun in Wales in 1859 and was then sweeping the country.

Rather than following his father into the ministry, the younger Stead chose a career in journalism. In 1871 W. T. Stead became the youngest newspaper editor in the country at the helm of the fledgling *Northern Echo* in Darlington in the north of England. He wrote to a friend, *". . . what a glorious opportunity for attacking the devil."* Britain at the time was powering through the industrial revolution. Capitalism had replaced paternalism. Corruption and immorality flourished,

The Least Of These

and poverty was more chronic than at any other time in England's history.

With God as his "senior partner," Stead rolled up his sleeves. *"I felt the sacredness of the power placed in my hands,"* he later wrote, *"to be used on behalf of the poor, the outcast and the oppressed."* Stead was determined to transform the *Northern Echo* into an "engine of social reform." One of his first editorials was on an issue that would have caused most decent Victorians to shudder with pious horror: prostitution. It was, he wrote, *"the ghastliest curse which haunts civilized society".* It was not the prostitute who offended Stead's Christian morality. In Victorian times, destitute women often had little choice but to turn to prostitution or face life in the dreaded workhouse. His criticism was aimed at a much higher echelon of society. *"Stylish houses of ill-fame,"* he thundered, *"could only be supported by men of wealth and respectability."* It was their "reckless passion" to which *"the ruin of the poor unfortunate is due."* Stead was playing with fire. Prostitution was not a suitable topic for daily journalism - the subject was tabooed by the press. But as a Christian he knew that he had to confront it.

In 1880 he left *The Northern Echo* to work for *The Pall Mall Gazette* in London. In 1883 Stead was given full editorship of *The Pall Mall Gazette*, which he immediately set about transforming from a lackluster gentleman's journal to a dynamic, even outrageous, political organ that soon became required reading for high society. His attack on slum housing in 1883 resulted in new housing legislation being drafted. In the following year his *"The Truth about the Navy"* campaign forced a reluctant British government to authorize funds to update and repair Britain's ageing ships. Stead practiced

Becoming Legendary

"New Journalism," which introduced into the British press such innovations as crossheads, illustrations, and the personal interview.

In 1885, Stead wrote the most sensational exposé of his career. Acting with several people, including his close friend General William Booth of the Salvation Army and Booth's son, Bramwell Booth, Stead uncovered a trade in child prostitution in the London underworld. He was shocked to discover that the government knew of the problem but turned a blind eye to protect the trade's wealthy clientele.

Enraged by what he discovered, Stead exposed the whole seedy business in a series of articles under the title *"The Maiden Tribute of Modern Babylon."* The story opened respectable society's eyes to the world of London vice: stinking brothels, fiendish operators, drugs, and padded rooms, where vicious upper-class rakes could enjoy *"the exclusive luxury of reveling in the cries of an immature child."*

The public outcry in London was unprecedented, even hysterical. The government was forced to enact the Criminal Law Amendment Bill which, among other things, raised the female age of sexual consent from 13 to 16. But engaging in good deeds can have consequences. As part of his exposé, Stead had staged the purchase of a young 13-year old girl named Eliza Armstrong in order to prove how easily impoverished children could be bought for immoral purposes. But Stead's actions - and those of his companions - left him open to prosecution for assault and abduction. He and several others were charged, tried, convicted and sentenced to prison, thereby paying a personal price for their Christian activism.

The Least Of These

Stead left *The Pall Mall Gazette* in 1890 to found the highly successful international periodical, *The Review of Reviews* where he continued to be controversial and outspoken, particularly about war. He was nominated five times for the Nobel Peace Prize. But in the year in which many people thought he would actually win the prize, W. T. Stead lost his life aboard *RMS Titanic* on the morning of April 15, 1912 while on his way to an international peace conference in New York. His body was never recovered.[48]

Good Deeds And Making a Difference

I am convinced that one of the ways that *"disciples of the Kingdom"* are to live out a faith which makes a difference is through our good deeds done in the name of Christ. Having given up on the institutional church, our Postmodern culture has concluded that it can manifest good deeds without Jesus. The Church, on the other hand, has concluded that it can manifest Jesus without good deeds. The world's plan seems to be working better than the Church's plan.

But I believe God wants to change this situation. In the coming move of God's Spirit in revival and spiritual awakening I believe God wants His people, including organic house churches, to become legendary for their good deeds.

---

[48]In recent years, more material has become generally available (thanks to the internet) on the life of W. T. Stead and the Elisa Armstrong case in particular. The Wikipedia article on Stead is quite good - http://en.wikipedia.org/wiki/Eliza_Armstrong_case. In 1972 the British Broadcasting Company broadcast a documentary on the Elisa Armstrong story.

Becoming Legendary

History reminds and warns us that every generation of Christians who are used of God, and every movement of the Spirit of God that moves beyond the four walls of the Church, is remembered for something. Legendary obedience is part of the legacy each generation of believers (both individually and as a Church) leaves behind them to encourage those who follow. That reality should come as an admonishment to the organic house church movement. We will all eventually be remembered for something. The only question is, "For what?"

Like one untimely born, I came to Christ at the tail-end of the Jesus Movement, a movement now legendary for it passion, power and hippie preachers like Lonnie Frisbee. I cut my spiritual teeth in a street ministry to G.I.s returning from Vietnam via Fort Bragg on the outskirts of my hometown, Fayetteville, N.C. I became a campus Christian radical at the University of North Carolina (Chapel Hill), helping to lead a campus-wide spiritual awakening there and eventually going on staff with Campus Crusade for Christ. *"You Campus Crusaders, why, you'd charge hell with a water pistol!"* bemoaned an exasperated pastor. Yep, it was the stuff of legends which still causes aging alumni to chuckle when reminded of those exciting days of "campus aflame."

When we look back beyond our own generation other legends stand out. During the Evangelical Awakening in England in the 1700s, John Wesley and the Methodists also became legendary. In an age characterized by debauchery and conspicuous consumption among the upper classes of English society, the early Methodists became legendary for their commitment to personal holiness and modest living. In an age of appalling child labor abuse and illiteracy, the

The Least Of These

Methodists became legendary for implementing "Sunday Schools" to give children a rudimentary education. In an age of poverty and debtors prisons, the Methodists became legendary for creating what today would be called "credit unions" to give the poor an alternative to pawn shops for short term loans and to help many of them start their own businesses. And in an age of widespread spiritual lethargy and social apathy, they became legendary for both their evangelistic and social work among the lower classes of English society, people excluded from or abandoned by the Church of England and the rest of proper English society. Every Methodist was required to pay a weekly "penny tax" which went exclusively to fund their outreaches to these people. Why were they willing to pay it? Perhaps it was in no small part due to the example set by Wesley himself, who became legendary for giving away 98% of everything he made through the sale of his books and writings.

When the vision for revival preaching and "cutting edge" outreach fell out of favor in the Methodist Church during the 1857 Awakening, a licensed Methodist preacher named William Booth, along with his wife Catherine, left the Methodist Church to found *The Salvation Army* and to recapture the vision of evangelism and outreach to *"the least of these."* As a result, new legends were created, such as Booth's work with London Journalist William Thomas Stead to expose the appalling social exploitation of child slavery and prostitution. These are people whom history remembers as "legends" when it comes to good deeds done in the name of Christ.

Becoming Legendary

Legendary? No!

There are other many other examples I could use, both historical and contemporary. I've used these particular examples in order to frame this question:

"What will you and the organic church which meets in your house become legendary for in the eyes of generations to come?"

I wish I could give you a clear and concise answer to this question, but I cannot. No one can. The answer will be determined by what each of us does in response to the call of God upon each of our lives. Anything I offer here is shear speculation (sanctified speculation, of course!). But since speculation on God's will for the future is a time honored tradition in the Church, allow me to share some of my speculations with you.

Let me begin by speculating on some things for which you will probably *not* become legendary for. I don't think we in the organic house church movement will become legendary for our structure. We will not become legendary for meeting in houses. Sorry. Organic church isn't about structure. It's about values.[49] And if you can't articulate those values, then you probably won't be doing organic church for very long.

Next, I don't really think we will become legendary for our

---

[49]Which is why we talk extensively about values in Chapter 4, *"Honey, I Shrunk The Church"* of our book ***Safe Houses of Hope and Prayer***, available on our website from Amazon.com

The Least Of These

books, magazines, newsletters, DVDs, or podcasts. Apart from his "Journals," are you familiar with any of the books John Wesley wrote (and he did a LOT of writing) or the name of William Booth's book,[50] or the magazine Evan Roberts edited after the Welsh Revival? Did Father Damian, a legend for laboring among the lepers of Moloka'i, even write anything (not that I'm aware of)? A generation from now will anyone even remember the book you are now holding in your hands? Don't count on being legendary for your writing.

And I don't think we will become legendary for our critiques of the traditional, institutional church and its perceived faults and failures. Do you recall the name of the Reverend Peter Price? Probably not, yet he created quite a sensation as the chief critic of the Welsh Revival of 1904. But today, when people speak of the Welsh Revival, they speak of Evan Roberts in terms bordering on reverence, not Peter Price. Unless they are spectacularly right, which they seldom are, critics generally do not attain legendary status, except as unwanted "gadflies."

Legendary? Yes!

Now, allow me to speculate about some things I believe God does want you and me to become legendary for in the coming move of His Spirit. By this point it should come as no surprise that I have a growing sense that God wants us to become legendary for our outreach to *"the least of these."* Legendary missiologist Lesslie Newbigin once observed that

---

[50]*In Darkest England And The Way Out*, and it is still available today.

Becoming Legendary

all thinking begins with a *"pain in the mind,"* and ministry to *"the least of these"* has become an inescapable *"pain in the mind"* for me. I believe there is a broader message here for the Church at large and for the organic house church movement in particular. This is no idle speculation for me. I serve on the board of a men's homeless shelter. I helped found a food rescue agency to supply food to the ministries in our city which feed those in need. And I have worked to see house churches planted in the toughest, most drug infested neighborhoods of our city. I believe God wants to take His available church "back to the streets" to reach out to *"the least of these,"* and He is looking for "legendary" believers who are willing to hear and answer the call. How this finds expression for you and your house church is what we are all waiting to see.

The Least Of These

Chapter 11

"My Brother's Keeper"

"True religion confronts earth with heaven and brings eternity to bear upon time. The messenger of Christ, though he speaks from God, must also, as the Quakers used to say, 'speak to the condition' of his hearers; otherwise he will speak a language known only to himself. His message must be not only timeless, but timely. He must speak to his own generation." [51]

In the generation since A. W. Tozer made the above penetrating observation, Christianity has (for the most part) squandered enormous resources of time, money and energy speaking a language known only to itself, while ignoring the universally understood "language of the Kingdom of God"; the language of God's love and compassion, embodied in good deeds done in His Name.

Christian philosopher and apologist Ravi Zacharias has posed the penultimate question of our day, namely, how do we effectively reach a generation of people who *"listen with their eyes and think with their feelings"*? I believe the answer is for each of us to "re-learn" this "language of the Kingdom" and to once again become legendary for our good deeds. By doing so, we will enable people of ths generation to listen with their eyes, to think with their feeling and to have open

---

[51]A. W. Tozer, **The Knowledge of The Holy** (London: Harper & Row Publishers, 1961), page 6.

The Least Of These

hearts and open minds to the good news of the Kingdom.

And that brings us to *"My Brother's Keeper."*

What Is "My Brother's Keeper"

"My Brother's Keeper" is an idea for a half hour television "reality" program demonstrating how Christians, Churches, businesses, ministries, agencies and people throughout community can come together to change the life of a person or a family in crisis. What if we as a community - particularly as a Christian community - could mobilize hundreds of volunteers, dozens of Churches, scores of businesses along with ministries and community agencies on an on-going basis to help real people solve real problems of hunger, homelessness, unemployment and many more practical issues which keep people stuck in their circumstances. Imagine bringing the people and resources together to help a homeless veteran or a homeless family get on their feet or helping homeless teens to get off the street and maybe even re-connect with their families. Imagine not just highlighting problems in our community, but actually solving them one person and one problem at a time. *"My Brother's Keeper"* is all about Christians working with their communities to solve real problems by serving others and *speaking "the language of the Kingdom."* And imagine creating a genuine model of solving problems by serving people, and then duplicating that model in communities all over the country.

A Philosophy For Becoming Legendary

"My Brother's Keeper" embodies a simple-but-profound

"My Brother's Keeper"

biblical truth: Sometimes the Kingdom of God tastes like a hot meal; feel like a warm blanket; comes in the form of a job offer, a Walmart gift card, a free car repair, a paid trip to the supermarket and a host of other acts of compassion and kindness. We've spent a considerable portion of this book examining the biblical teaching and importance of good deeds in the life of the professing believer. All of that teaching can be summed up in an underlying philosophy which stands behind *"My Brother's Keeper."* That philosophy was best expressed 250 years ago by John Wesley, leader of the Evangelical Awakening in England, founder of the Methodist Church and a legend when it came to good deeds and speaking *"the language of the Kingdom."* He expressed it this way:

> *"Do all the good you can,*
> *by all the means you can,*
> *in all the ways you can,*
> *in all the places you can,*
> *at all the times you can,*
> *to all the people you can,*
> *as long as you can."*

Now, THAT is a philosophy for becoming legendary, and it is the unspoken-but-universal language of the Kingdom of God. The philosophical goal of *"My Brother's Keeper"* is to demonstrate the love of God toward people in need and to do it in practical ways which they can understand and appreciate within the context of their own life-struggles. In the process, we want to highlight the positive role that believers and churches can have and the positive contribution they can make in addressing and solving the practical problems which affect the lives of those around us.

The Least Of These

Five Specific Goals

Now, in addition to having a catchy philosophy, a project the size of *"My Brother's Keeper"* needs some specific goals. We have five:

1. To Help - First and foremost, we want to provide practical help for real people in crisis. The "big idea" here is to identify specific practical problems which are keeping real people and families stuck in their particular life-crisis. Once we have identified the people and the problems, we want to rally Churches, ministries, agencies, businesses and people to offer practical help and solutions.

2. To Highlight - Next, we want to highlight those Churches, ministries, agencies, businesses and people which are making a difference in the community by serving people and solving problems. The "big idea" here is that there are people and organizations in our community which are actively helping people to solve practical problems. We want to give them the positive exposure and support they need and deserve.

3. To Stimulate - Do you remember *"Good Deeds Principle #15: Stimulate One Another"* which we explored back in Chapter 4? The third goal of *"My Brother's Keeper"* is to stimulate greater community involvement in serving those in need. Yes, it's time to "incite" and "provoke," just as we learned earlier. Why? Because people need both the motivation ("stimulation") and the opportunity to "do the right thing." And because we need more people at the table. There are people throughout our community who, if given the

"My Brother's Keeper"

opportunity and a little encouragement, would step up and get involved serving those in need in our community. We want to offer them opportunities to get involved.

4. *To Raise Awareness* - The fourth goal of *"My Brother's Keeper"* is to raise public awareness of specific widespread and chronic issues which affect quality of life within our community, including, but not limited to, issues such as hunger and homelessness (we currently have initial plans for episodes of "My Brother's Keeper" dealing with ten different issues, and that's just for starters!).

5. *To Give Back* - Our final goal is to raise financial resources, above and beyond the cost of producing *"My Brother's Keeper,"* which we can sow back into the lives of people in need and ministries which are serving people and meeting needs.

An Idea Whose Time Has Come!

"My Brother's Keeper" is a biblical idea whose time has come. Every major city and community in America is looking for practical approaches to doing real good and solving real problems. The good news is that, today, more and more people are looking for practical ways to do good and to make a difference in their communities. "My Brother's Keeper" could give them both the encouragement and opportunity they've been looking for. Why not bring together the best people and ideas that our community has to offer in order to solve real problems for real people. People understand doing the right thing for the right reason and serving other people. I can only imagine what would happen if more people and

The Least Of These

Churches stepped out of their comfort zones and got more involved doing the right thing. What a great opportunity for Christians to take the lead in doing good (just as we learned in *"Good Deeds Principle #9"* in Chapter 4) and bringing our communities together to help people and solve problems.

A Video Reality Project Unfolds

When fully developed, the plan for *"My Brother's Keeper"* is to produce a one-half hour television "reality" show documenting issues of hunger, homelessness and a wide variety of related issues. The program will showcase how a Churches and communities come together to address a chronic social issue by changing the life of a person or a family in crisis. The plot and procedure of each program (with variations) will unfold along the following basic outline:

What? - The exposé - This is the stage of the program that develops and explains a specific widespread problem that affects our community (for example, homelessness among men, including military veterans; homelessness among women with children and the lack of shelter space for women in crisis).

Who? - The Personification - In this part of the program we will identify and introduce a specific person (or family) who is struggling with this issue. This person will have been pre-selected and screened through a recognized organization experienced in working with this particular population. We want to assure that the need is legitimate and to establish a level of confidence regarding their ability to succeed moving forward. Through a process of pre-interview we will

"My Brother's Keeper"

determine some of the underlying issues and needs which, if met and resolved, could put this person on a path toward long-term success.

How? - The Implementation - This is where we will bringing together a combination of Churches, ministries, agencies, businesses and individuals (who have agreed to participate) to help address the issues which have been identified. At this point in the program we will introduce positive solutions to the practical problems which have kept this person or family stuck in their circumstances and unable to move forward.

Sample Program Plot

The following is a fictional sample plot of a possible "My Brother's Keeper" program. I include it here for illustration purposes.

The program theme is "homeless families" and the opening 5 minutes of the program documents the plight of homeless families in our community (and elsewhere) and the extent of the problem. The *"My Brother's Keeper"* team assembles at a café venue and participating business in north Spokane to discuss the problem and how we can help with the solution. The focus then narrows to the Juarez family (a mom, dad and two kids). They came to town pursuing job prospects which fell through. When their resources ran out they ended up sleeping in their car and eating at a local ministry serving free breakfast out of a Church basement. We interview the director of the breakfast ministry about what they do and who comes through. As the program progresses, the Juarez family is taken in by a faith-based ministry which works with

The Least Of These

and provides residential shelter for homeless families. We interview the director who talks about what they do and who comes to them. Together we interview the Juarez family. We discover that the dad has some job prospects, but is hindered by lack of suitable work clothes and no reliable transportation because their car has broken down. They can't get out of the hospitality network until they have enough money for deposits and rent. Working with local churches and agencies *"My brother's Keeper"* finds and presents the following solutions: A local private garage owner agrees to help out by towing and fixing their car (for free) so they will have reliable transportation. A small participating church offers to take up a special offering and take the Juarez family clothes shopping for new clothes. A local realtor and property manager agrees to help find suitable housing for the family, while a larger participating church decides to take up an offering and pay all deposits, rent and utilities for the family for 6 months while they get on their feet. They will also take them grocery shopping. The program ends with a "job well done" discussion among the team and a discussion of how people in the local community watching the program can volunteer and get involved helping families in crisis.

The Incredible Potential of "My Brother's Keeper"

"My Brother's Keeper" will be examining issues and solving problems which are present in communities all over America from Hawai'i to Maine, and from Alaska to Florida. In addition to the immediate benefit of helping people in need throughout our community, we believe *"My Brother's Keeper"* presents us with some amazing opportunities and incredible potential:

"My Brother's Keeper"

1. The potential exists to reproduce the program and its model in communities coast-to-coast as a successful tool for rallying local communities to address and solve chronic social problems.

2. It presents us with an opportunity to inform and motivate large numbers of new people concerning the practical issues and needs within our community and how critical their own involvement could be in helping to meet those needs and to address those issues.

3. It presents us with a unique opportunity to change the public perception of Christians and Churches as uninvolved and uncaring regarding the practical needs of struggling people in our community.

4. It presents us with a unique opportunity to express the values and good news of the Kingdom of God in practical terms which are intrinsically good, outwardly attractive and easily understood by those who witness and experience them.

5. It presents us with a unique opportunity to offer interested viewers practical opportunities to respond and become involved in good deeds throughout their community.

6. It presents us with an opportunity to raise funds, above and beyond the cost of producing the program, to sow back into the lives of people in need and to support the work of ministries which are making a difference.

The Least Of These

Here's How You Can Step Up And Get Involved!

Are you ready to become legendary?! If what I've shared so far interests you - even excites you - then consider this your invitation to get involved and to make a real and tangible difference in the lives of people in need. This is your opportunity to be part of something bigger than yourself; to serve those in need; to become "legendary" in good deeds; and to make a difference for the Kingdom of God. Here are some specific ways you can get involved right now!:

1. Tell Your Story! Let's start by making this personal. Perhaps you are like the lovely lady at the Rental Car Agency I introduced earlier (see page nine). You have a personal story of struggle, faith and overcoming adversity (unemployment, homelessness, drug addiction, etc.) that no one else knows. You may even think your story isn't worth telling; that no one would be interested. We disagree. We want to hear your story. As part of our *"Everyone Has A Story"* Project, we are looking for real people who are willing to tell their unique stories of how their life journey has brought them to where they are today. We want to publish the best and most compelling of those stories in a series of books tentatively entitled *"Everyone Has A Story."* This is your opportunity to tell your story! You can learn more on our website (risingrivermedia.org). Click the *"My Brother's Keeper"* tab in the menu and look for **"Everyone Has A Story."** You'll find all the details on how to submit your story.

2. Tell Us About The Good Deeds You Are Involved In! You may be one of those "shining lights" of the Kingdom who has been involved in "doing good" to those around you

"My Brother's Keeper"

without telling anyone or making a "big deal" about it. Or perhaps your Church or ministry has been at work doing good. We want to hear stories of your personal involvement. Again, go to our website (risingrivermedia.org), click the *"My Brother's Keeper"* tab in the menu and look for *"Everyone Has A Story."* You'll find all the details on how to submit your story.

3. Challenge Your Church To Become Involved! We're looking for Churches, ministries, businesses and individuals who want to bring their unique gifts and resources to the table to serve people in need and to solve specific problems.

4. Become A Financial Partner! We can't do this alone. We need your help and participation. We're looking for financial donors, sponsors and advertisers who want to be a part of sponsoring the production of *"My Brother's Keeper."*

5. Volunteer! We're looking for volunteers willing to donate their time as support staff to help with such things as legal work, accounting, research, script writing, advance production work, technical production and editing, web production and more.

Learn more on our website:

www.risingrivermedia.org

www.ingramcontent.com/pod-product-compliance
Lightning Source LLC
Chambersburg PA
CBHW051422090426
42737CB00014B/2779